Paupers, Dukes a

Hooke – *A West Dorset*

Duncan Harris

Duncan Harris
14th September 2005

Line drawings and maps by John Anderson

Published by
Barnes Publishers
4 Barnes Lane
Beaminster
Dorset
DT8 3LS

First published in 2005

ISBN 0-9550294-0-6

To my wife, Patricia, for her encouragement, support, love and help over 44 years.

Printed and bound by
Creeds the Printers, Broadoak, Bridport

Contents

Preface

At school, history focused on the British Empire, it was a subject full of dates and names to be remembered. The idea of being able to find local information, ask people for their memories and relate these to documentary evidence was far from my concept of history at that time.

My interest in history began when I lived in Bath for nearly 20 years. I became an academic in another discipline, learning the use of books and papers to put together a case.

When we moved to Hooke in 1994, I thought that a book about how Hooke evolved would be interesting. I was amazed how much information was available, and also how much was missing. I gave myself 10 years to try to put together the story. The evolution of the landscape was a fascinating study for the Hooke valley, with courses at the Kingcombe Centre including one with Oliver Rackham to whet the appetite.

How did the village become as it is today? There is much documentary evidence from the Manorial Court records. Unfortunately, the church records were destroyed along with those of many other Dorset parishes in the fire at Blandford Forum in 1731. Records show that the churches of the village were there in the 14th century. The detail that may be accessible to other writers about villages is clearly not available here. I have had to make some guesses and some extrapolations that may later be proved incorrect if further records come available. However, it seemed to me that a fuller story, with clear indications of when supporting evidence was available and when it was not, was preferable to a story with many holes in it.

No doubt there will be others who can fill in the gaps and also come across further evidence, both documentary and on the ground: Hooke has had little archaeological work done, and, like many Dorset villages that are primarily pasture and meadow there has been little disturbance of the ground. I hope that somebody else will extend the ideas and correct some details that will no doubt be in error. In Chapter 2 I have made many suppositions. Purists may wish to omit Chapter 2 from their reading! Later chapters have more supporting evidence.

To help anyone else interested in following up this book most of the notes that I used are in Beaminster Museum in the history files.

I would like to thank my wife, Patricia, and the many people in Hooke who encouraged me and provided a large amount of information. The project unearthed about 150 photographs that may be enhanced for some sort of ultimate access and details of over 50 Boer War officers who convalesced at Hooke Court (details of whom have already been produced as a separate publication).

Duncan Harris
Beaminster 2005

Acknowledgements

There are many people who have helped this publication to come to fruition: John and Ena Anderson, Canon Tim Biles, the Reverend Rose Bullock, Reg Bush, the Cornick family, John and Theresa Colton, Peter and Mandy Cooper, Derrick Crocker, Dorset County Library, Dorset County Museum, Dorset Record Office, Babs Draper, Jane Draper (whose dissertation on the child of the nineteenth century ... Parish of Beaminser gave useful insights), Bob Edwards (whose dissertation on the archaeology of Hooke gave me a flying start), the late Marie Eedle, Joy Edwards, Jessica Featherstonhough, Anita Fursey, Pam Lemmey, Brian and Gill Haynes, Allen and Sheila Hill, Mr. Hillman, John and Joyce Hunter, Trevor Hutchings of Taunton,the Reverend Ken Masters, Dr Jane McSherry, Cina Parker, Mary Payne, Roger Peers, the late George Pinney, Richard Pinney, Margaret O'Shea, Dr Murray Rose, Jane Rose, John Earl of Sandwich and Caroline Countess of Sandwich, Julian Skotzen, Roger and Gill Smith, Bernard and Pauline Wallbridge, Brian and Val Wallbridge, Bernard Webster and many others whose names I never knew.

I would particularly like to thank John Anderson who did all the maps and line drawings. The readers of the earlier versions: Jenny Cuthbert, Babs Draper, Pam Lemmey, Ken Masters and Jane Rose for their many valuable suggestions respectively:

- Questioning the idiosyncracies of my cut and paste technique, where the paste had occurred and the cut had not and picking up a myriad of missed spelling by Spellcheck and myself;
- Correcting some of my local and detailed assumptions about Hooke in the last 50 years;
- Identifying my over enthusiasm for unsubstantiated suggestions about potential historical ideas;
- Correcting some of my ecclesiastical and church terminology and assumptions;
- For an amazingly detailed range of suggestions for improving my phraseology, structure and presentation in English!

My wife checked the final version, any remaining errors are either deliberately my decisions or unintentional.

I apologise if I have inadvertently omitted somebody whose name I should have remembered. I can only offer the excuse of age.

Duncan Harris
Beaminster 2005

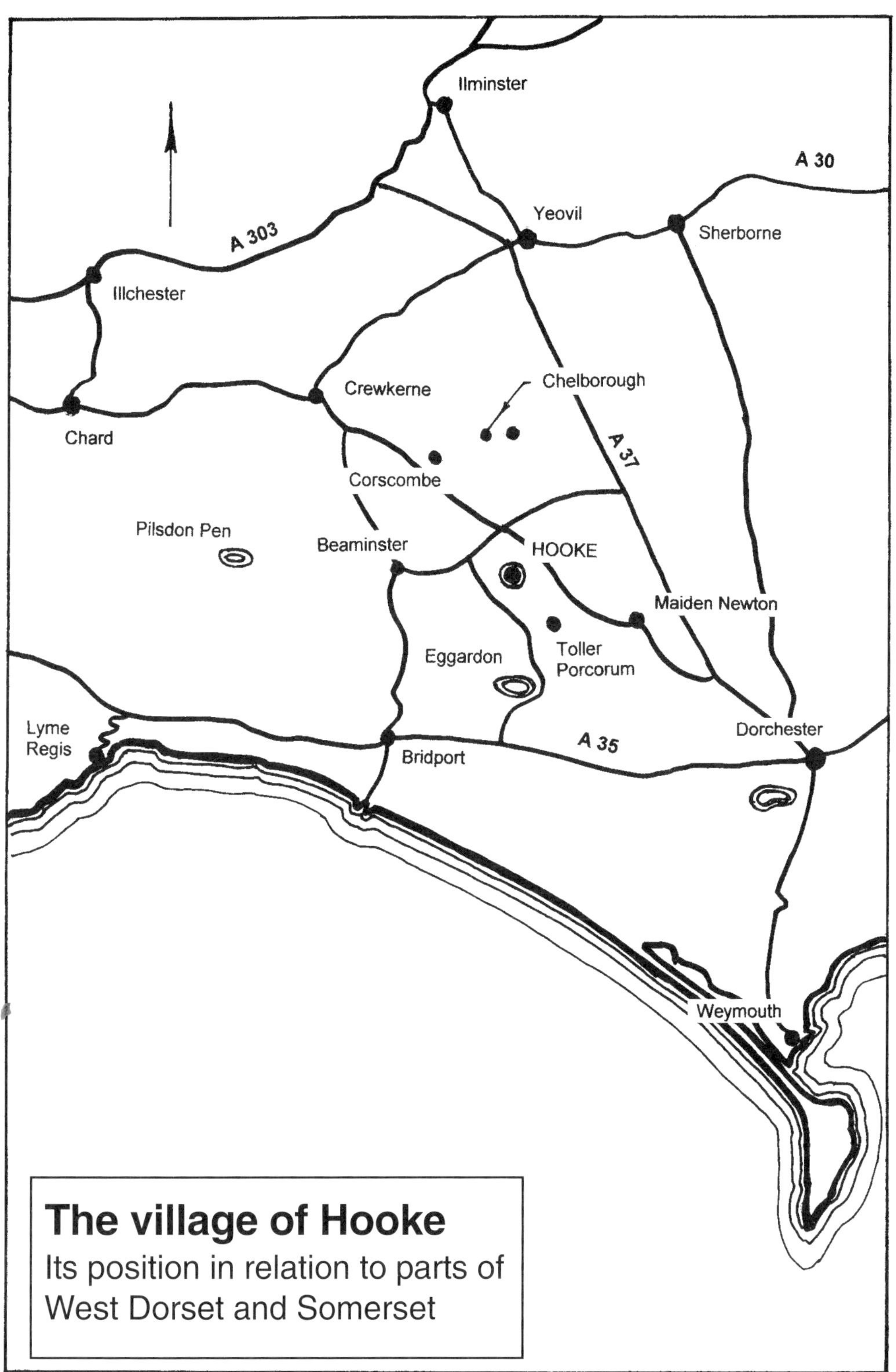

The village of Hooke

Its position in relation to parts of West Dorset and Somerset

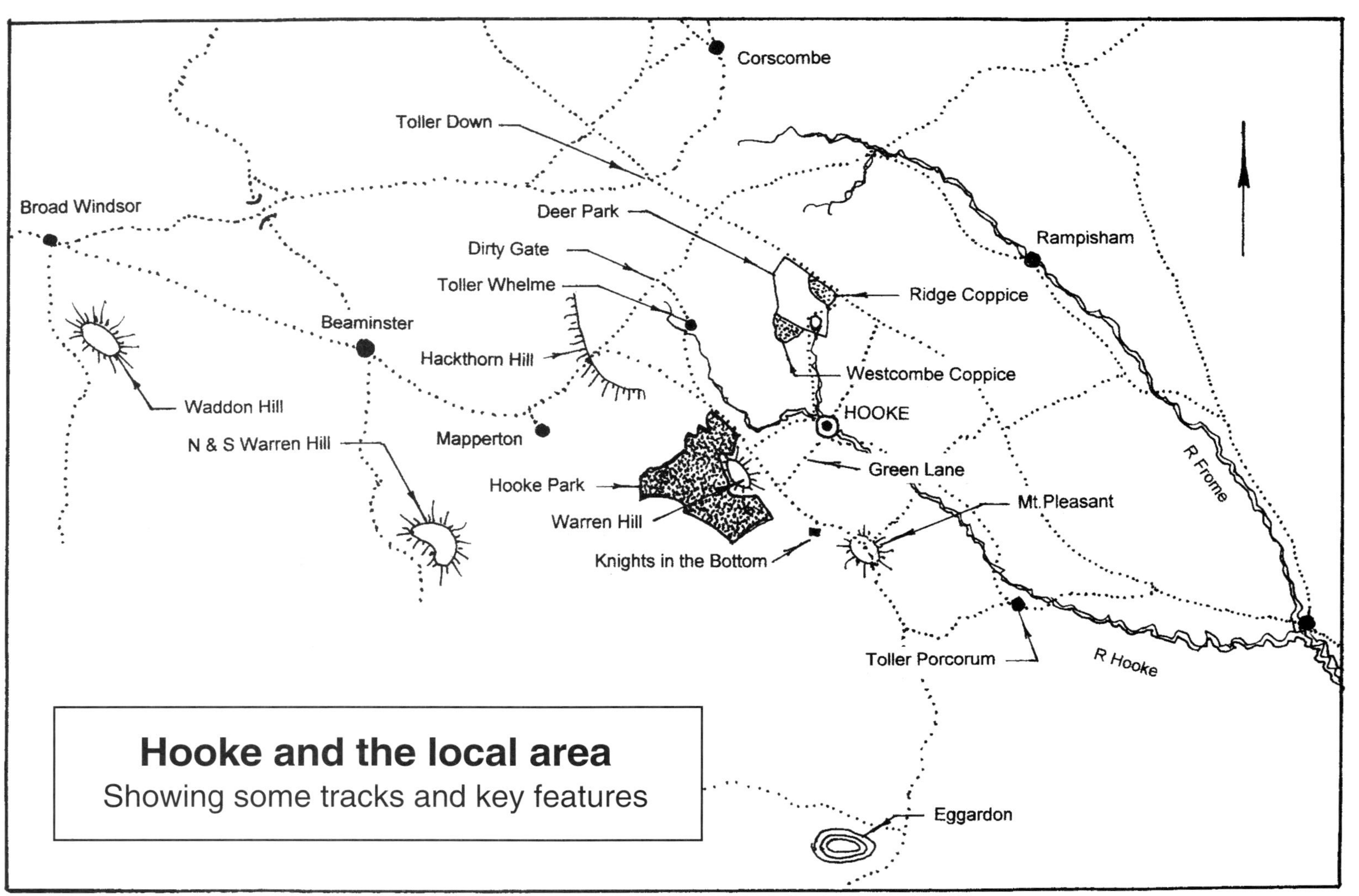
Corscombe
Toller Down
Broad Windsor
Deer Park
Rampisham
Dirty Gate
Toller Whelme
Ridge Coppice
Beaminster
Hackthorn Hill
Westcombe Coppice
Waddon Hill
HOOKE
N & S Warren Hill
Mapperton
Green Lane
R Frome
Hooke Park
Mt. Pleasant
Warren Hill
Knights in the Bottom
Toller Porcorum
R Hooke
Hooke and the local area
Showing some tracks and key features
Eggardon

Chapter 1

Introduction

Hooke is a small village in West Dorset with a current population of about 130. The nearest small town is Beaminster. The village is in the valley that runs from Toller Down to Maiden Newton, where the River Hooke joins the River Frome.

Its name derives from the 1086 name for the village La Hoc. The Old English *hoc* means a projecting corner, sharp bend in a stream. The name suits the topography well.

Structure

River

The village lies near the head of a valley leading to Maiden Newton. There are several hamlets and villages along the valley, Hooke, Higher Kingcombe, Lower Kingcombe and the largest, Toller Pocorum. The River Hooke that flows down the valley helps to make up the River Frome at Maiden Newton, flowing on through Dorchester to Wareham and out into Poole Harbour. The River Hooke is one of the River Frome's more important and yet lesser-known tributaries.

The River Hooke has several sources, most being springs, one at Toller Whelme and about 16 in and around Hooke, one being described by an author (Ralph Whiteman) as the largest that he had seen. South of Ridge Coppice, by Park Pond is a horseshoe of very boggy country, which nourishes a fair flow of water, which in turn is augmented by a rivulet from off Pipsford Farm.

Geology

Moving north from the Bridport area the rocks are a mass of sediments from the Jurassic age. There were frequent earthquakes, faults, uplifts and down-thrusts giving the peculiar set of valleys and hills below the chalk down land. The geology of the area in the parish of Hooke (just over 1250 acres) is very varied. There is a wide range from chalk on the downs to clay in the valley with outcrops of greensand and several other rock types. A detailed geological map and relief map are shown in the figure 1.1. Fuller's earth is quite common along the Hooke valley and also plenty of greensand and clay.

Above the Exogyra sandstone are developed the Chert beds that first appear from Maiden Newton through Hooke and Toller Whelme to the eastern end of the Axe valley. A fault acts as the floor of the valley of the River Hooke from Langdon to Higher Kingcombe. The fault gives rise to the higher beds of Upper Greensand on the north rather than the south side of the valley. There is a fault line along the Gault slopes of Warren Hill and Mount Pleasant.

Chert beds form the north-eastward sloping plateau between a point on the side of the road about 600 metres south west of Hooke Court and Hooke. There is a considerable thickness of glauconite sand and is capped by chert. About 1000 metres south by west of Hooke Court the chert beds may be seen on Warren Hill on a natural exposure.

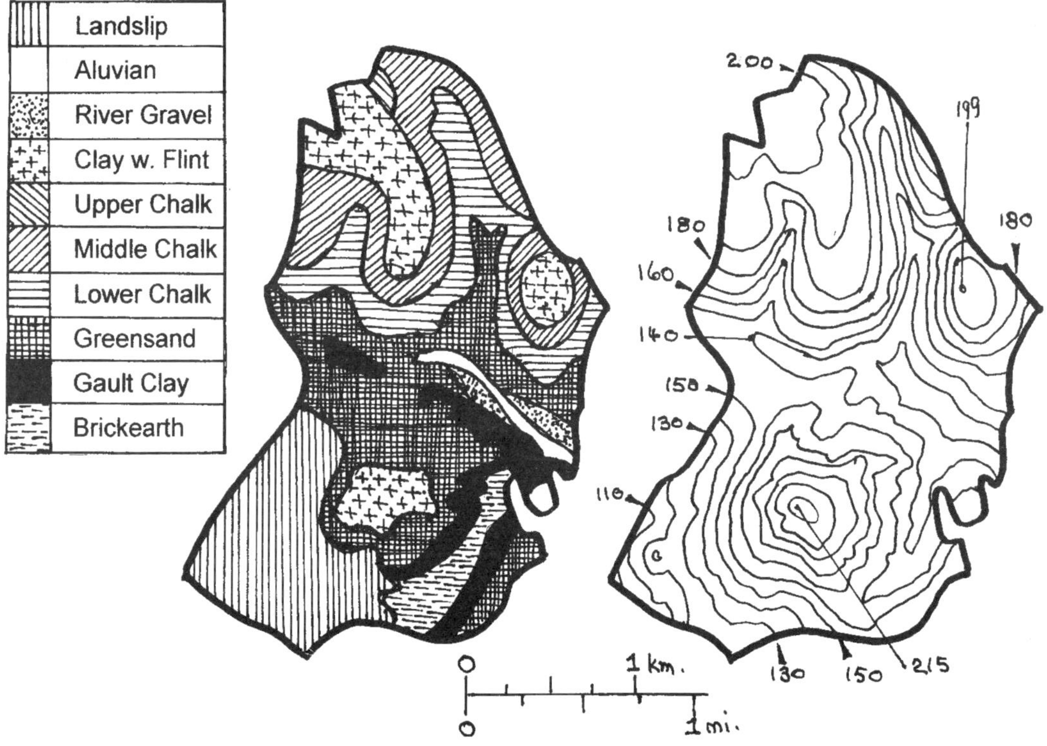

Figure 1.1 **Geology of Hooke Parish**

There is a large landslip on the Greensand escarpment between Hooke and Beaminster that is 2.5 miles long. The slip probably occurred at the end of the glacial period when the land surface was cracked by the frosts and the cracks filled with ice. On melting the whole surface, clay and greensand alike, slid on a curved slip plane whose lower edge coincided with the valley bottom. There are many minor more recent landslides along the Hooke valley giving a sequence of features in fields going down the slope of dry at the top, wet in a trough, and dry on a rise from the slip. Such fields have a wide range of grasses, reeds, sedges and wild flowers. There are small landslips like this in many fields, probably occurring in the last 200 years. Where these occur most of the fields are used as pasture, although recent work has partially levelled and drained one large field in the parish that has been replanted in the rye grass monoculture.

Boundaries

The boundaries follow roads, streams and field boundaries. Hooke Park may have originally been part of Powerstock Forest. The ecclesiastical connection with Powerstock appears in about 1437 when Hooke first gained the right to bury its own dead in the parish rather than at Powerstock. The original Hooke Park, mentioned in detail later, is now spread across two parishes: Corscombe and Hooke, suggesting that some of the present parish boundaries may date from about the 17th century, after the Commonwealth. Earlier boundaries may have followed the roads and the streams more closely than at present.

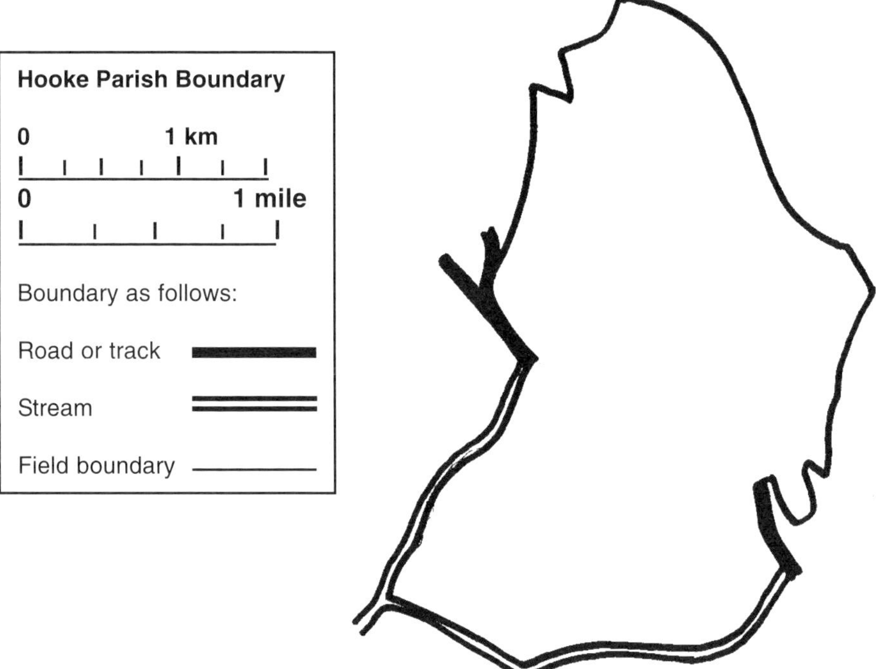

Figure 1.2 **Parish Boundaries**

Roads

Probably the oldest road is that leading from Beaminster Down along the top of the village at Warren Hill, down through Knights-in-the-Bottom. The road was the Dorset Ridgeway that joined up with the Great Ridgeway that went from East Anglia to Wessex. The Dorset Ridgeway linked up with the great Iron Age forts at Eggardon and possibly Maiden Castle and pre-dates those hill forts. It was probably the route used later by the Romans when they advanced to Exeter over a two-year period.

Such an ancient track within a few hundred yards of the current village and a copious supply of water suggests that there were some early settlements nearby, although evidence is lacking. The valley would have been partly marshy and much of the current valley shows the work of man in capturing and using the water. It is my opinion that the Romans with their excellent water engineering may have been interested in such an area, but more of that later.

The village appears to be based on the two nodes of track junctions of about eight tracks. Thomas Hardy, in his novel *Under the Greenwood Tree*, seems to have Gabriel Oakes living at Hooke at the beginning of the novel and also moves a turnpike gate into the village instead of its actual position at Toller Down.

There is also a puzzle. According to records there were originally two villages, the second being Stapleford. The parishes of Stapleford and Hooke were merged in 1361. Where was Stapleford? One theory is that the two parts of the present village were the two separate villages. There are different ideas about which part of the current village was which village. One suggestion is that the part of the village with Hooke Court was the original Hooke and that the part of the village with the church was the original Stapleford. It is possible that the church of St. Giles stands on the site of an earlier church, possibly Stapleford church. However segments of documents from the 14th century refer to Westhoke, but there is no mention of Easthoke. If the latter existed the two parts of the village are accounted for. A further possible site of Stapleford is Knights-in–the-Bottom. It is also a junction of tracks. There were several houses there even in the 19th century and there is some evidence from foundations of a building in a field that there could have been more. The name Knights-in-the-Bottom seems to occur first in the 19th century.

People and Interactions

Hooke was a village dominated by the local lord of the manor. The Manorial Court was held in a manor house (Hooke Court) with a moat that still exists in part today. It was primarily an agricultural village and a poor parish until recent years. In the 20th century it had a large watercress farm and more recently a trout-breeding farm. The copious supply of water was not only being used by these enterprises, but also tapped for water supplies in 1963.

The village today has lost its school, pub, shop and Post Office. Its cricket club is shared with Powerstock and no longer plays at Hooke but at Nettlecombe. It still has its church, part of the Beaminster Team of 12 parishes. Village Parish Meetings are held in the church or in Hooke Court. In spite of no obvious community facility the great outdoors enables barbecues, garden fetes, line dances and bonfires. About one quarter of the adult population work in the village and about another quarter go out to work from businesses based in the village. Several of those working in the village and going to work from the village are self-employed. In 2003 the age distribution was from two new babies to an 88 year-old. The proportion of retired population is below average for the UK. At the beginning of 2003 there were over 30 youngsters under 18 out of about 130 people who live in the village.

Agriculture

The village is an area of the country that is identified as ancient countryside rather than planned countryside. There are hedges, mainly mixed not straight, most roads are not straight and many are sunken, there are many public footpaths. Enclosure did not happen through an Act of Parliament, but by agreement of the landowners in the valley as early as the 17th century.

Chapter 2

Pre-History to the Norman Conquest
(Up to 1086)

National Background and Village Structure

Nationally

The period covered represents English history from the Stone Age, through the Iron Age, leading on to the Romans and then Saxon times! Over this period there were frequent changes of rulers that may or may not have had an effect on Hooke.

One of the Dorset branches of the Great Ridgeway ran from Beaminster Down to Eggardon. It leaves west of the tumulus on Beaminster Down. It crosses Hackthorn Hill at Dirty Gate where it follows a green track (marked by a sign "Route to a public right of way") that joins the minor road to Hooke. It winds over Warren Hill, through the valley and up to Mount Pleasant. Most of the down land would have been woodland and scrub that had become intensively cultivated in the early Iron Age. The route would have been an ancient trade route and linked to other tracks leading to the hill top camps along the ridge over Beaminster to Pilsden Pen. The original link may have been pre-historic with origins similar to those of the Great Ridgeway.

Hooke

In 4500 BC the area in which Hooke stands would have been wild wood dominated by lime, a tree almost unheard of today in the area. A big lime tree would rot at the base and fall down but new growth would emerge from the stump.

Early people would need water on journeys along the Ridgeway (Figure 2.1) and would need to replenish it at regular intervals. The water initiating from springs at Hooke would be clean, but may have been hidden in woodland or marsh. It is likely that animals would have found this copious supply. Individuals would follow animals to find such a supply and may have built small platforms to enable easier access. There would be little likelihood of tools being needed other than to construct and maintain such a platform.

There have been no Stone Age or Iron Age tools, flints or other evidence found to date in Hooke. Such remains have been found at Lower Kingcombe further down the valley where the water would have been more accessible. However, Lower Kingcombe is much further removed from the ancient trackways (see map on next page). The reason that no tools or flints have yet been found may be because there is a large platform stretching from the East of the current site of Hooke Court to its West, such disturbance would have been a major piece of civil engineering. Whenever it was carried out it is likely that any remaining artefacts would be distributed and even buried under several feet of earth. A further reason is that most of the parish is woodland, pasture or meadow and has been for a long time. The ground has not been disturbed and artefacts would be unlikely to be found on any but the arable land.

An occasional ploughing of pastures enabled a large number of fragments of Roman tiles to be found dating from the second to fourth century. These tiles were in two fields to the north west of the village. It seems possible that these were used at that point for a villa or farm dwelling. The site faces south at the top of a slope. The nearest known Roman villas were at Halstock (which used stone tiles), possibly at Rampisham (little remaining evidence) and Maiden Newton. It was unusual but not impossible for such tiles to be transported from one manor to another for secondary building purposes (e.g. a sheep shed, see next chapter). There is clearly a possibility of some Romano-British presence in the village.

The Roman influence would have been a small villa or more likely a farm and such a building might have been very simple. It could be the Romans who first constructed a platform for building a residence and outbuildings on the site of the current Hooke Court but no remains dating from this period have been found. There was a Stall House to the north west of the village in 1840 with a large well nearby in the field below the site. There could have been a previous well in the same area but nearer to the possible Romano-British building described later.

Land was bought in order to make money from sale of crops to towns. Dorchester (Dvrnovaria), and Ilchester (Lindinis) were the nearest known towns. The distance from Ilchester did not deter the rich owner from building the large Halstock villa. Dorchester would be the more likely for Hooke, being just over half a day's ride away. The owner might have been a lesser Roman official, a retired soldier, or even a successful local person in the Roman administration. Some locals would have worked the farm. Villages often derived from such small origins. The land would have been fertile, it had a good supply of water with springs and wells available and there was a good supply of timber making it quite an attractive proposition. An alternative is that the possible farmhouse could have provided for the local villas but until some more evidence is found it remains a conjecture.

There were probably thousands of individual small farms in the pre-Roman Iron Age. The changes brought about by the Romans would have been considerable; there was stability of life; there were excellent main roads and a network of minor roads; there were market towns; there was money so farmers could sell surplus crops and buy slaves, hire servants and labourers, and could have obtained the services of expert craftsmen to build to Roman patterns with Roman materials that would have been locally produced. These farmhouses represented a development in the standard of living. The building could have been simple rather than elaborate. The farm would probably have been a tenancy; so a tenant would not be likely to invest large amounts into repairing a building. In much of the country in the fourth century there was inflation and instability that may have prevented owners or tenants investing in the repair or maintenance of buildings.

It is possible but unlikely that the mill could have originated from the Roman times, although there is no firm evidence. Certainly the technology to provide leats, sluices, water wheels, both undershot and overshot, existed in Roman times. In addition, the general use of water from springs was a normal Roman undertaking, such water being considered easier and purer than from any alternative sources except wells.

There was a house and a mill in the village during Saxon times. The house would probably have been on the current site of Hooke Court, although again no artefacts remain. Twelfth century pottery sherds have been found in the field opposite Hooke Court to the North and some evidence of buildings. The mill would probably have been on the site of the current white house the other side of the large ornamental pond at that end of the village; certainly this was the site of the mill until the last century. It was near the many springs where the flow was probably largest and the route of the water would have been adjusted to ensure maximum utilisation. The Park Pond may also have been built with a dam in order to ensure a steady flow. Mill wheels at that time would probably have been undershot, the Roman technology of

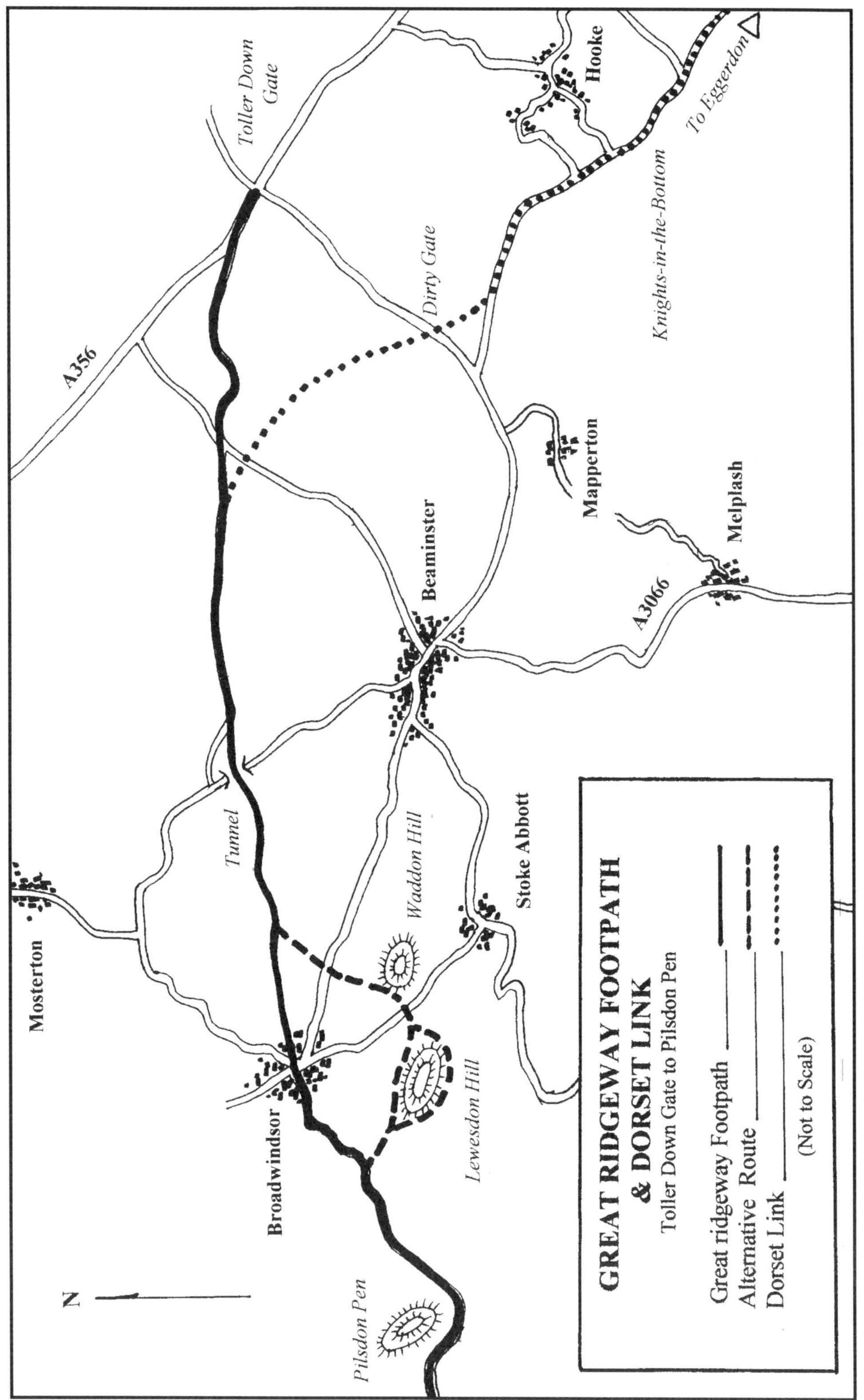

Figure 2.1 **Great Ridgeway and Dorset Ridgeway**

overshot having been lost. Flow rate rather than height was important and being a chalk stream there is a good flow all the year round. The source of some of the springs is reputed to be from Salisbury Plain.

The manor house and the mill would probably be wooden at this time, possibly with thatch for a roof, with a good supply of reeds nearby (there are still reed beds near to the site of Hooke Court). These buildings would have been infested with rats and mice from the earliest times.

Domesday entries, when compared with other manors locally, suggest a small, relatively poor manor with the mill being the only significant comparable entry.

Christianity

A closer relationship between Christianity and the state occurred during the time of Constantine. By the beginning of the fourth century there were three bishops for Britain. Patronage by the church had become important and powers were transferred to the church from the Roman magistrates. There were rich Christian landowners, backed by favour from the imperial house that presented the Roman governor with limitations when he had to take into account the wishes of the church and its officers. Clearly there were political as well as other implications to be considered by any tenant or owner in Hooke.

By the third quarter of the fourth century the roads were in a bad state of repair and the barbarians had infiltrated Britain. The towns were fortified, but the countryside had become a fearful mess with small bands of raiders looting, destroying, taking prisoners and killing at will. It was probably during this period that the end of any successful farm at Hooke occurred. By 410 there were problems of payment to Roman troops and evidence that they had been withdrawn to the continent. The local administration would presumably still have involved some of the Roman ideas and ideals. The victorious West Saxons incorporated the system of government that included post-Roman influences from the church with monasteries having an important role. The structure of society for the Celtic monks had changed little since the Roman occupation.

Dorset became accepted as part of the Christian establishment in 705 with the appointment of a Bishop of Sherborne whose see was carved out of the old Wessex diocese. In 1075, following the decree of the Council of London, which ordered the removal of sees to more populous areas, the see was moved to Old Sarum and subsequently to Salisbury.

How was Christianity introduced to Hooke? It probably started with an itinerant preacher (a monk) who would have set up a wayside cross at a crossroads. Eventually a wooden church with a thatched roof could have been erected or possibly two: one in each village. It would most probably have been near or inside the manor house, or associated with its buildings. No evidence of such buildings has come to light, although it is possible that the current church, probably the first with stone walls, could have been built on one of the sites.

Individuals of Interest

Pre Domesday the hundred was called GLOCHRESDONA and became Eggardon Hundred. "Aluric held La Hoc in King Edward's time." The taxation rates shown in Domesday would have originated from this period.

The village was called Lahoc at this time (Hoc 1091-1106; Hoch 1155; del Hoc 1200; del Hoke 1244, Hoke, 1235-6; Houk(e) from 1346, also La Hoke 1244-1369). There are two different local views about the meaning of Hoc: oak or in Old English 'projecting corner, sharp bend in a stream' both of which fit the topography of Hooke. Most publications tend towards the latter view. At the time of the Domesday Book (1086) the tenant-in-chief was William, Count Mortain, half-brother of William the Conqueror. He was the greatest landowner in Dorset and probably the richest man in England apart from the king. It was assessed at 2 hides. "There is land for three ploughs. There are two ploughs in the demesne, with one servis, four villains and three bordars with one plough. A mill pays 6s (shillings) and there are 6a (acres) of meadow, five quarentens of pasture and four quarentens of wood. It was and is worth 40s." Hoc was in the Hundred of Eggardon. The tenant (sub-tenure) in 1086 was William de Lestra, in 1166 Richard del Estra, in 1212 Richard de Atris, in 1235-6 William De Letre who are all the same family. In 1285 Stapleford was also shown in the hundred when Roger Arundell held it. Stapleford may be a name of Durotiges origin. The Domesday Book does not include Stapleford, but there is a manor of Roger by William "the Goat". The size would be 6 hides, 1 virgate and 3 acres. Those calculations are made by Eyton to make up the missing part of Eggardon Hundred in the Domesday Book!

Stapleford in 1084 was held by Roger Arundel (Rogerio Arundel) and the sub-tenant was William Capra (Willelmus Capra) according to the Inquisitio Gheldi, whose identification with specific Domesday manors has been thus to more or less facilitate (Eyton). This estate appears to have been omitted accidentally from Domesday.

Stapleford was called Stapelfow (1244, 1285), Steplford (1360, 1385, 1447), and Stapylfow (1471). The name means a ford marked by a staple or post (Old English Stapol, ford).

Interactions affecting people in the village

The Roman 2nd Legion obviously had a difficult time advancing against the Durotiges. According to one author (Field) the Roman advance took the route from Eggardon along the old Dorset Ridgeway with variations to the current lanes Figure 2.2. It took two years to advance from Wareham to Exeter. There is a straight hedge from Knights-in–the-Bottom towards the top of Green Lane that Field identified as a section of the Roman route. It is unlikely that an army advance route would be built as a permanent road. In 2003 there was an investigation by County Council historians that the bank there may support the suggestion. The causeway from the end of Green Lane was dug only to find some evidence of a clay route across the line, but no hard core along the line.

There is a known camp at Waddon Hill. Field argues that the road (roughly the current road across Warren Hill to the village boundary) was used to begin the move to Waddon Hill and also became the military route to Exeter from Dorchester. The army collected fresh vegetables and water en route. The site at Hooke would have been good for growing vegetables on the slopes each side of the valley. The Romans were excellent water engineers. The copious supply of water would have required little ingenuity, by Roman standards, to be stored and used. As has already been stated there seems to have been at least a Romano-British farm at Hooke. Such farms occurred at regular intervals along the route.

Agriculture

Neolithic man came in around 4000 BC and brought crops and animals. Much of the wild wood was stripped for pasture and arable land. The conversion of wild wood to farmland would have been completed over a very long period of time by 500 BC at the latest. The appearance of much of the countryside originates from these times.

Neolithic man may have used the chalk down land as they were particularly attractive and suitable for Emmer wheat and barley. The land would have been lightly covered with trees and bushes so it was easier to clear them compared with heavily forested clay lowlands. It could be that some of the down land was originally wood pasture where Neolithic man took livestock into clearings in the wildwood. These farmers kept sheep, cattle, goats and pigs and grew flax to provide linen. On the downs there is some evidence of use with the Hoare Stones at Toller Down (possibly the remnants of a Neolithic long barrow). Clearing the down land of vegetation gave pasture and arable land, important for the Dorset economy. It also enabled craftsmen to provide tools and instruments. In the Iron Age there were iron works nearby at Tollerford.

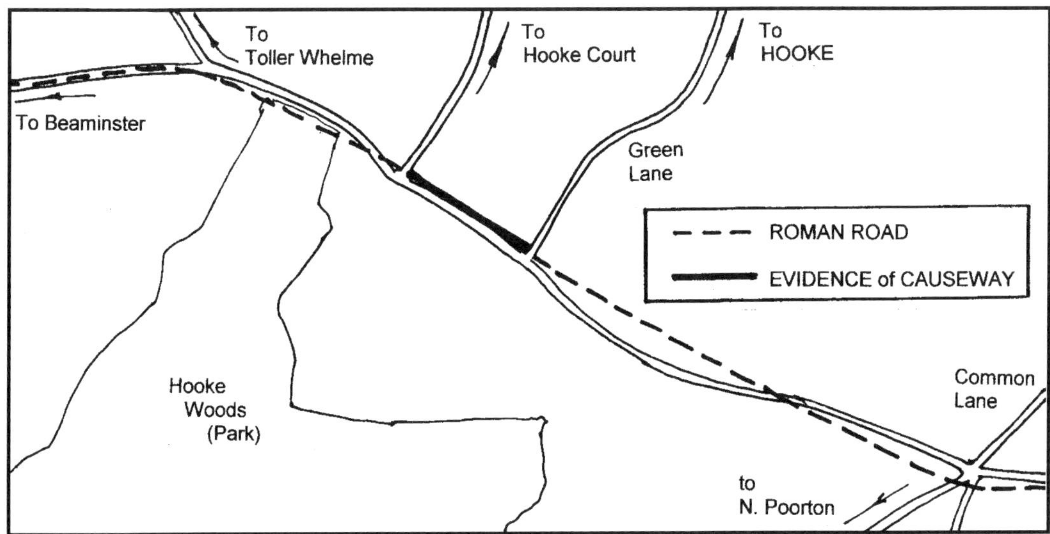

Figure 2.2 **Possible route of Roman road near Hooke** (according to Field)

By the Iron Age more robust tools and therefore complex structures were possible. Animals may have been driven down to the valley to drink; the nearness of the valley would make this likely. Roe deer would have been killed for food and are still plentiful around Hooke, probably more so now than they have been for centuries. On the north slopes are outlines of square Celtic fields (about 1.5 acres and rectangular). These could date from pre-Roman to a much later period. Cultivation with a plough would have caused these squares because the action of the plough tends to move the earth down the hill.

The agriculture at the time of Domesday was woodland (a good source of income), a little pasture and meadows.

Chapter 3

Early Owners of Hooke Court and the Cyfrewasts (1086-1390)

National Background and Village Structure

Nationally

There was civil war in the time of Stephen, the nephew of Henry I. The countryside was ravaged, crops were destroyed and cattle driven off. It seems unlikely that Hooke would have escaped these national problems. The civil war involved Matilda, Henry's daughter. The next king, Henry II (Matilda's son), had castles built and there were taxes, never popular. Judges and 12 local men were to administer justice in the shires, so Dorset had a new administrative system for justice. The king appointed clerks and Thomas à Becket queried the royal power. The term "clerks" ranged from archbishops to vergers and accounted for about 1 in 50 of the population.

Richard I spent about 10 months of his 10-year reign in the country, but required revenue for the crusades against the Moslems. His successor John was supposed to be the typical "wicked" king, reported by some as cruel and avaricious, although there is some doubt about this reputation. He built a motte and bailey castle at Powerstock and hunted in Powerstock Forest, so clearly would have had an influence in Hooke!

Hooke Court and village

All the documents referring to Hooke at this and later times show Hooke to be in the hundred of Eggardon. Many of the old maps of Dorset and some old and more recent books give Hooke in the hundred of Beaminster, a mistaken description.

By the late thirteenth century there was a major building on the Hooke Court site with a moat. Much more excavation and the extension of the platform would have occurred. The owners were the Cifrewast family (spelled a variety of different ways). The family had permission to crenellate in 1344, in the reign of Edward III. The moat appears to have been rectangular from the parts that still exist (see Figure 3.1) and enclosed about 2.3 acres.

Most moats date from the 12th or 13th centuries, but the one in Hooke is later. Moats were relatively unusual in Dorset compared with Eastern England. Permission was given in the reign of Edward III in 1344. Moats had begun to go out of fashion about 1325 for the higher echelons of society, but yeomen were beginning to incorporate them. It seems unlikely the Cifrewasts were yeomen; perhaps Dorset was always behind the times in catching up with what was fashionable? There may have been a bridge and the ground inside the original moat was raised, probably with the earth and stone that was dug out of the moat. A supply of water would not be a major problem in Hooke (the remainder of the moat still has plenty of water in it without any obvious external supply)!

The building would probably have had a cross passage with an open hall on one side and a buttery and pantry on the other, leading to a separate kitchen. Beyond the hall would have been a parlour and possibly a room above called a solar. A licence for crenellation was an important status symbol. It usually meant that there was some connection with the king and also that the owners were rich. The moat was probably constructed at the same time with a defensive wall alongside, the house being within these walls. Later versions of Hooke Court had a wall of the building alongside the moat. The northern arm of the later 15th century building went to a point about 30ft. west of the present west range. The western part of the moat was filled in and there are now no traces except a marked sinking in the carriage drive just east of the entrance gates.

A stone with a gryphon carved into it has been found in the grounds and is probably from the front door surround of the building, the gryphon being the symbol for the Cifrewasts. The stone is on display in the main building of Hooke Court. A diagram showing the likely position on the door frame is in the church at Hooke.

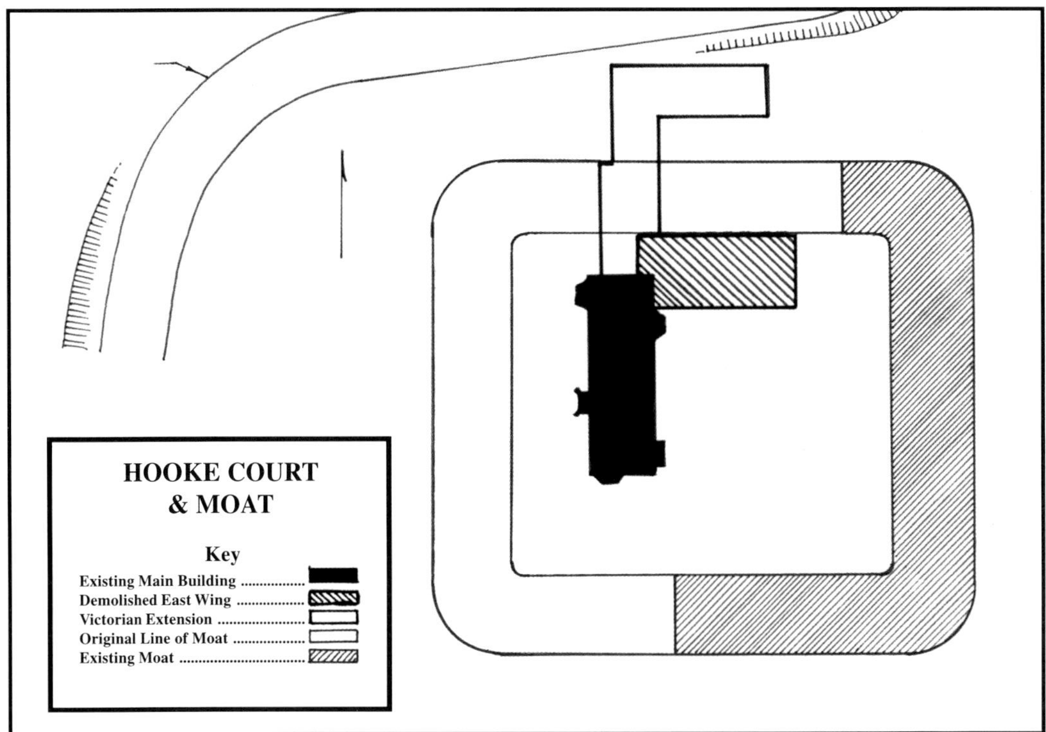

Figure 3.1 **Plan of Hooke Court and moat**

There are two remaining manor houses of this period still in existence in Dorset: Woodsford Castle and Moigne Court. Woodsford Castle has considerable details of the building in the 14th century. Here advantage was taken to create an impressive defensive house with all the important rooms on the first floor and there were towers in corners. Moigne Court only had permission for a wall but no crenellation. The design of Hooke Court seems to be in between the two extremes. With our knowledge of the current site, the layout of the rectangular moat, and the two contemporary manor houses in Dorset we can only make conjectures. An artist's impression of how Hooke Court might have appeared is shown in Figure 3.2.

It is clear that by the beginning of the 14th century Hooke had become an important village with a moated, crenellated manor house and a dovecote. A dovecote was an expensive building, usually circular and made of stone. It could house over 1000 birds. The dovecote was not only a prestige symbol but also provided precious dove dung for enriching the kitchen garden. The dovecote suggests that there was a group of buildings and emphasises the importance of the owner as only a Lord of the Manor of higher status would have the right to build it. The cost of construction would have been beyond the reach of an ordinary man. A moat gives an indication of the possible size of the house and other buildings at that time so there were probably many buildings around the courtyard although there are no details.

Further evidence of the importance of Hooke Court occurs in 1361: "Inquisition taken at Cerne, Wed. In Easter Week ... Hoke and Stapleford. A messuage, dovecote, two carucates of land, 13a of meadow, 60a of pasture, 50a of wood ... of the King in chief by service of a fourth part of a knights fee."

Figure 3.2 **Artist's impression of Hooke Court in the 14th century**

A dagger of the 14th century type was found along with two smaller knives and a key when the moat was cleared out in about 1960. These artefacts are held at the Dorset County Museum.

Mills

In Anglo-Saxon times (and even Roman times) earthen dams were built to provide a good water supply to mills. It seems possible that Park Pond originated as a feeder reservoir for the leat to the mill. According to one source Park Pond was installed in 1380. Was this a new development or an expansion of the feeder reservoir to the mill to serve a second purpose as a water supply for the deer park? The work carried out would suggest that there might have been an expansion of the deer park at this time. The pond was dammed to provide a good supply of water. The pond and the dam have been recently renovated.

The main product from the early water mills in Hooke were cloth (the fulling mill sited where the present white house is on the other side of the small lake near Hooke Court) and flour from a grist mill (the location is less certain but there was a later hemp and thread mill behind the now Paulet House and a mill behind the two bungalows by the bridge on the Toller end of the village). There appear to have been no windmills: surprising in view of the surrounding hills.

Stapleford

Stapleford was granted a market and fair in 1239. Stapleford does not appear to feature much in the documents after 1244 other than jointly with Hooke such as in the Lay Subsidy Roll of 1332, although the manor gets a mention in 1399. One author (Good) suggests that the Hooke Court end was Stapleford and the other end of the village was Hooke, but his argument is based on the building of Hooke Court in 1400, whereas it had been in existence for nearly 100 years by then. It seems more likely that Stapleford might have been where the scatter of houses and the church are at present, but the next evidence casts doubt on this location.

West Hooke

At some time there was a Westhoke. Deeds held by the Harvard Law School Deeds Project include three entries: "about 1290 a John le Gale quitclaim his right to ½ furlong of land from Robert de Stockeye in Westhoke." On June 26, 1325 "Gilbert de Westhok, son and heir of Amulph de Westhok grants a messuage and all his land in Westhok (Dorset) to Roger le Hore." On December 8, 1328 "Sonota, widow of Roger le Hore quitclaim to John de Barkendon 1 messuage and a furlong of land." On January 8 1329 "William, son of Sonota de Hoke, granted ½ furlong of land and 1 acre of meadow in Westhoke (Dorset) ... to John de Berkedene which he had of the gift and feoffment of Roger de Hore of Westhoke". On August 21, 1369 "William de Barkadon was granted an annual rent of 60s (shillings) to be levied on all his lands at Hoke to Niel Loryng."

Churches

The first record of a rector is in 1312. There seems to have been some dependence on Powerstock. In 1338 Robert Cifrewast had to take his grandson to Powerstock church to be baptised. By 1362 the rectories of Hooke and Stapleford were consolidated. Presumably there were separate parishes and possibly churches or chapels. There is a mention of a chapel at Hooke in 1330. Dorset was particularly badly affected by the plague in 1348 and 1349; that may have reduced the populations of the two villages. One source states that the clergy of Hooke and of Toller Porcorum died in 1348 and links their deaths to the plague.

The sites of the churches are not clear at this time but the new church was built at the beginning of the 15th century possibly on the site of one of the existing churches. There is a suggestion that one of the churches was dedicated to St. Giles; he was the patron saint of wayfarers, cripples, and blacksmiths (see Appendix B). It was normal to leave bread and water in the porch for wayfarers. He is also associated with animals because of the legend with the hind saved.

Tracks and Communication

In medieval times the route up Rampisham Hill continued over the hill, through Knapp Farm towards West Chelborough. The route out of the village in the other direction went up Green

Lane; there being no route through Hooke Court until the 19th century. There would have been paths: tracks to almost every habitation, and between them, and into most fields. In 1890 (Ordinance Survey map) there were still many footpaths, some of which no longer exist. The tracks between villages were known as "king's way" (*regia via*), lesser ones were "church way", "common way" and so on. The flooding of ways was a major problem and Manorial Courts considered this the main road offence. It would have been a general problem in the Hooke valley and no doubt ditches were maintained to ensure less flooding - no longer the case in the 21st century - such is progress! Other problems included leaving wood, earth, muckheaps, and dead animals on the highway. The highways were part of common land of the manor and were specified in detail. Encroachments were a problem (one such occurred in Salway Ash where a house was built across the highway!). If there were any bridges they were probably footbridges across the river. The other crossings would be fords of which there were probably at least three: one in what is now Knights-in-the Bottom, one on the road from Toller Porcorum, one at the bottom of Mill Lane. The roads such as Mill Lane and Green Lane are the original medieval routes, along with the road through Knights-in-the-Bottom that has already been identified as of ancient origin.

There are several holloways (deep cut lanes through soft rocks) that occur in Hooke. The erosion would have occurred through the use of horses and horse drawn vehicles followed by water flow through the channel made in the soft rocks. The holloways include Green Lane, Mill Lane, the bridleway above Park Pond, the bridleway from Chalk Corner towards the radio masts, the road going out of Hooke towards Higher Kingcombe, the bridleway from Manor Farm towards Common Lane and the road along the edge of Hooke Park.

The current road from Toller Down into Beaminster is a turnpike change. The original road led from Toller Porcorum and Hooke up to Toller Down Field and then on to Corscombe. There was a road to Mount Pleasant along the old Dorset Ridgeway and another to Toller Whelme. There was a further road from Mapperton through Coltleigh to Hooke Court. Other routes were through Burcombe and Hooke Park to Hooke Court; from by the mill near Hooke Court, up Mill Lane and across by the current radio masts; a further road was the one mentioned earlier to Rampisham Hill and continued across the new main road and towards Knapp Farm. An important route that no longer exists went along close to the valley where the Hooke rises by Park Pond (currently a Bridleway) on to the Green Hut and Corscombe. According to Good (1966) at least six roads radiated from Hooke, so the current roads are old.

There would have been two roads through the valley each side of the river. There are few remnants left on the South side at the Hooke end. Hooke was the principal road centre in the vales with two nodes, one by the church and the other by Hooke Court. Hooke became a backwater after the opening of the turnpike roads. Although the turnpike road is shown as a continuous road from Maiden Newton to South Perrott on Taylor's map of 1811, the southern part of it was still incomplete as late as the second decade of the 19th century. The coach road from South Perrott to Maiden Newton was still through Mosterton, Beaminster, Hackthorn Hill, Hooke, Lower Kingcombe and over the hill to Chilfrome. The local landowners still had to maintain the roads.

Pottery finds

12th century sherds have been found in addition to medieval sherds in various parts of the village. The map (Figure 3.3) shows their location (after Edwards 1994).

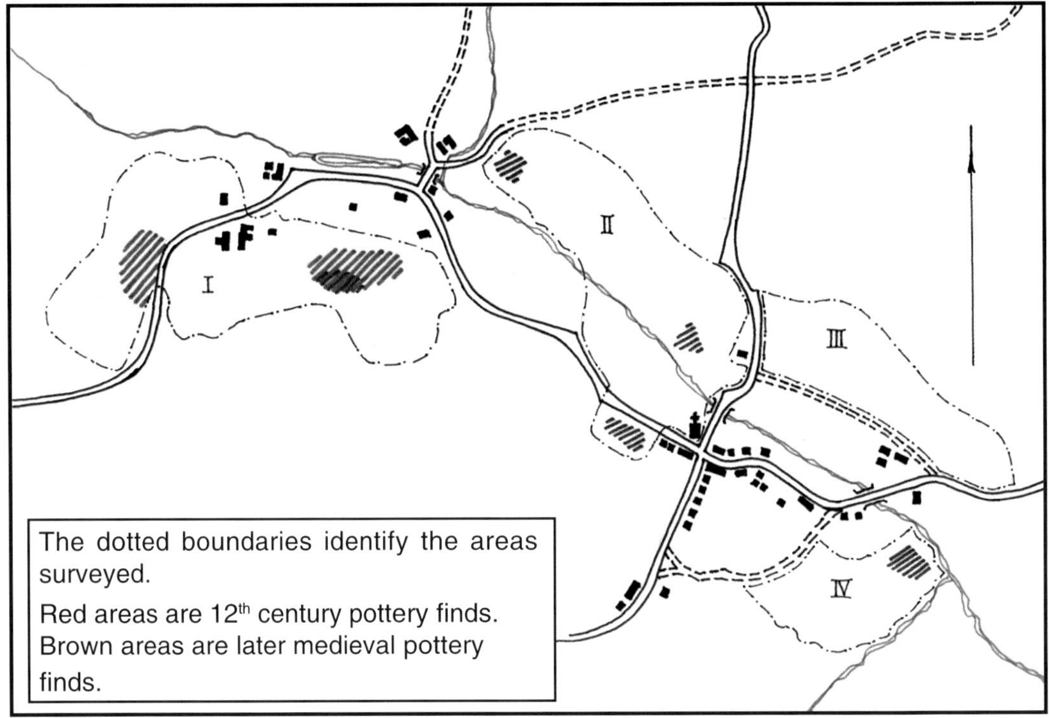

Figure 3.3 **Sherds found during excavations (after Edwards 1994)**

Individuals of Interest

Owners of Hooke Court

The chief tenant was still "Morton" in 1235, but the tenant was William de Lestre, who was required to pay aid for the marriage of the king's sister. The king at this time was Henry III. The king would have been 28, having come to the throne in 1216 when he was 9. By 1239 Stapleford had a licence to have a market and fair.

In 1285 Stapleford was also shown in the hundred when Roger Arundell held it. The Domesday Book does not give a size but it could have been about 6 hides, 1 virgate and 3 acres (according to calculations to make up the missing portion of Eggardon hundred in Domesday).

One owner of Hooke in the thirteenth century was William Lestrange, but little else seems to be available on current searches. John Molindar de la Hoke is recorded in 1274/5, but it is not clear whether he is chief tenant or tenant. The family still had a presence in Hooke in 1332 when Radulpho Molendinario was one of 14 inhabitants taxed for 12 pence or more. The owners of Hooke later in the thirteenth century were the Cifrewast family. In 1281 John de Cyffrewast held la Hoke; John his son, aged 4 was the next heir. By 1315 the owner was Robert Cyfrewast (what had happened to John?). The Cyfrewast name (spelled a variety of different ways e.g. Sifrewas) was that of a knightly family in Hampshire, Dorset and Somerset and also occurs in Dorset specifically at Portesham and at Combe Almer, near Sturminster Newton (in the Lay Subsidy Roll with the same spelling as at Hooke).

The Sherborne Missal was the greatest survival from the great library at Sherborne Abbey prior to the dissolution of the monasteries. The illuminator-in-chief was John Sifrewas, a Dominican friar who ran a workshop probably in London. The work was produced under the joint patronage of Richard Mitford, Bishop of Salisbury (1396-1407) and Robert Bruyning, Abbot of Sherborne (1385-1415). John Sifrewas did many excellent illuminations at that period and often included himself in the pictures. His self portrait and his family crest are both shown in the Sherborne Missal. John Sifrewas, presumably, came from the same family.

One source suggests that the Mautravers family (from Henford in Somerset) held Hooke from 1342. Hutchins identifies Sir John Mautravers as being of Hooke. He died in 1386 and was buried at Abbotsbury. Mautravers' widow was Elizabeth who married Sir Humphrey Stafford, being his second wife, who presumably came to be the owner of Hooke Court soon after 1386. Coker says that Humphrey Stafford who married Maltravers heir was the great builder of Hooke Court.

Hok and Stapleford have 14 entries in the subsidy roll:

Hundred of Ekerdon
Hok and Stapleford

Robert Cyrewast	6s 8d	William Loppe	12d	Galfrid Bonewyle	9d
John Stour	12d	William Colyer	3d	John Robyn	12d
Ralph Molend	12d	John Upgreve	9d	Thomas Louote	12d
Ph Bcar	12d	Michael Marteford	10d	John Porar	12d
John Gagy	12d	Thomas Werthog	2s		
				Total	22s

Neither John Pavely nor John Stapleford, the two clergy, appear on the list. Clearly Robert Cyfrewast was the rich man of the villages. The patron of Hooke at this time (from 1312) was Gafrid de Corington.

Interactions affecting people in the village

Big heavy things, like millstones, were being transported to remoter parts of England from later Saxon times. The conveyance could be a cart drawn by up to eight horses. A cart of this type would do 10 to 15 miles in each day. The lord of the manor had rights to demand cartage from their tenants. Tenants' carts would often carry brushwood and manure for the lord. Maintenance of roads and bridges was a responsibility for all. In 1285 the Statute of Winchester placed an obligation on all landowners to maintain the highways passing through their manors. A toll could be charged for passing on these roads. However, road mending was an irksome duty and not generally carried out; any tolls collected were often pocketed for private use. Magna Carta excluded the building of new bridges, so bridges were unusual for villages. Highways and paths were often boundaries in Saxon Charters, although a few of Hooke's boundaries are along paths or roads on the 1890 Ordnance Survey map. Perhaps some field boundaries may have been older routes.

John de Molendinar, that is John the miller, at La Hoke (Hooke) in the reign of Edward III went to Wyke (near Gillingham in Dorset). John bought a millstone from the miller there. The miller at Wyke was the miller to the Earl of Gloucester. I imagine that John brought the millstone back to Hooke with some difficulty. Meanwhile Stephen, the bailiff to the Earl of Gloucester, found out about the purchase. He came to the fields in the Hundred of Ekerdon (Eggardon) and removed cattle belonging to John and drove them to Lindeton to the manor of the Earl. John was required to pay 20s (shillings) fine for the return of the cattle. Stephen maintained that the Earl's miller had no authority to sell the millstone.

There are some unanswered questions:

- Did John pay his fine?
- Did he get his cattle back?
- Did the Earl know what was going on?
- Was Stephen making some income on the side?
- Was there any restriction placed on the bailiffs?

Certainly a fine of 20 shillings was a lot of money for a miller. Did he go into an early-day bankruptcy? We shall never know! The information comes from a case about the extortion by bailiffs.

John de Paveley was rector of Hooke from 1312 and Robert Syfrewast gave custody of his belongings to the rector. The idea was that the inheritance was safe for Robert's son because a rector should have been trustworthy. The sheriff was required to go to Hooke in 1315 because John, the rector, had destroyed a sheep house worth 100s, cut down and sold 37 apple trees, 8 ash trees, 300 whitethorns, and uprooted 1000 alders. All these had brought in 700 shillings. The sheriff did nothing, saying that the writ came too late! In the same year John also sold a house and its surrounding land, a garden, 2 lots of land, 9 acres of wood and 10 acres of alder. Needless to say, these all belonged to Robert. This time no price is given, but John was becoming quite rich.

The following year (1316) the sheriff had to come to Hooke again for the same matter. Presumably the writ arrived in time because some action was taken. It was normal practice for 12 people to carry out the investigation. The report was duly written but did not state whether John and Robert were present. In addition there was no statement about who carried out the investigation. The case was dismissed because of these omissions. It almost looks as though John and the sheriff were related!

The sheep house mentioned in 1315 may be where the Romano-British tiles were found in 1998 at the top of a field. It was not unusual to re-use tiles for buildings such as this.

Robert and his wife Joan had a further brush with the law in 1330. Simon Sifrewast appears to have brought a case to court because 2 messuages, 2 mills, land and rent in Hooke, Benville and Charminster to the total value of 17s 6d was his. One Thomas de Lutteswell represented Joan. Robert acknowledged that Simon had the right to these. Simon granted them to Robert and Joan for their life.

Lord of the manor, Robert Syfrewast, made "a present of a doe in his park of Hoke" to a witness of the baptism of his grandson in Powerstock Church in 1338. So it seems possible that there was a deer park in 1338.

Church

The rector of Hooke and the vicar of Toller Porcorum were both reputed to have died in 1348 from the plague. Many vicars succumbed to the plague after giving the Last Rites. Robert Cifrewast became patron in this year. It seems likely that the populations of all villages were considerably reduced. The Black Death killed half the population of England. It may have had the same effect on the populations of the two parishes of Hooke and Stapleford. The two parishes were united by order of the Bishop of Sarum in 1362 because they were considered too small. The name Stapleford eventually disappears completely. The separation of the two parts of the village may originate because the lord of the manor built a village for the workers away from the manor house to reduce the possibility of the transmission of the plague.

Tithing was in place. The tithing was a unit within the vill (village) and in Hooke commensurate with the vill. Here the reaper was attached to the tithingman who was responsible for the whole tithing, breach of the peace and robbery. The Dorset reaper (often called mensor) was apparently a person of considerable importance, and elsewhere acted as rent collector. Possibly the reaper was attached to the tithingman in Hooke to limit any extortion and violence.

Entertainment

Entertainment could include some seasonal mumming plays done by villagers, usually involving St. George fighting the Turks and a doctor coming to heal those injured. This form of entertainment was common in Somerset, the border of which is a few miles from Hooke. Such events took place in Beaminster and probably also in Hooke. The plays would probably be similar to those still taking place occasionally in Beaminster during its annual Festival.

Agriculture

The agriculture at the time of Domesday was woodland (a good source of income), a little pasture and meadows. Hooke would have been largely alder trees near the water and probably oak trees on the less waterlogged ground. The valley and the hills have been cleared of trees at various stages. The date of this clearance is not obvious although much of it will have occurred by about 1200. By 1250 there may have been more pasture land (much of it wood pasture) and certainly more meadows. There may have been quite a lot of common land roughly from Green Lane to Common Lane. Much of the pasture would have been the chalk down.

The Normans probably introduced fallow deer to the area, along with boar. Fallow deer could provide meat from poor quality land. Fallow deer have probably been here ever since; the white deer of the Eggardon herd would have been popular with the king visiting Powerstock Common in later years. Deer parks multiplied in the twelfth century. There is no hard evidence of a deer park in Hooke until the fourteenth century, but it could have been there longer.

Fishponds were quite common in medieval times as a source of food. Fish farming (which still occurs in Hooke with a trout breeding farm) provided a good source of food. The fishpond at Hooke Court probably dates from this time and the dam appears to be an earth dam to a stream that feeds the pond. The pond, dam and stream have recently been renovated.

It could be that Warren Hill was dug out for rabbit burrows at about this time, medieval rabbit being more delicate than the animal known today. Like fallow deer, rabbits provided meat from poor quality land. They would not have become pests until the late eighteenth century.

It is possible that by 1338, the year that a doe was given (as referred to earlier), a substantial deer park was in existence, but small enough that deer could be rounded up by dogs and netted for food. The alternative source of the fallow deer to be found in West Dorset today could have been the fallow deer in the deer park. The deer pale consisted of a bank and a ditch on the inside. The width of the ditch and the bank varies around the park judging by the remnants left today. Deer can leap about 15 feet length and clear about 6 feet vertically. The bank had a hedge at its top, or more likely at Hooke a set of palings made of oak. The idea was that the deer could not jump out of the deer park because of the ditch and fence, but deer from outside could jump in to replenish the stock! The outside boundary allowed 15 feet clear to enable timber to be cut and the pale to be repaired.

There may have been a house for the deer ranger on the site of the agricultural buildings (stall house) shown on the tithe map of 1840. The site certainly would have had an excellent view of the deer park, with Park Pond also in view. Such a small park would not only have been for a supply of venison and other meat, but also to supply wood and timber. The other meat could have been wild swine, wild bulls and hare. Venison was no ordinary dish; it was a special dish for feasts and honouring guests. That may explain the possible expansion and mention of the park from the time of the Cyfrewasts to the Paulets.

Agriculture would have changed considerably from 1348. The rapid decline in the population (which would not recover for another three or four hundred years) would require fewer fields that had been ploughed for food. The strip approach to ploughing on slopes may well have gone out of production.

Chapter 4

The Staffords

(About 1390-1460)

National Background and Village Structure

Nationally

Richard II was still king at the start of this period of the village's history. There had been a Peasants' Revolt in 1381 based on price rises and wages being restrained. There was unrest and Richard was murdered in 1399. The usurper Henry IV became king amid continuous rebellions. It is interesting to note that Henry IV died in 1413, as did the owner of Hooke Court Humphry Stafford and also Humphry's wife! The next king, Henry V, was pious, stern and a skilful soldier. He renewed the war with France and had he lived for another two months he would have become King of France, but in 1422 Henry VI became king at the age of 9 months. In 1428 Joan of Arc was a difficult opponent in France. Henry suffered from madness in 1454, when Richard became Regent, but Henry had recovered by 1455 during the War of the Roses. He was still king when Hooke changed hands.

Local government

The Statute of Westminster set up the Justices of the Peace in 1361. The function of the Justices of the Peace became an effective system of local government and justice over the next 300 years. The well-off gentry lived in their manor house, enjoying the comforts that their tenants' rents provided. They also exercised their powers as magistrates and Justices of the Peace not only locally in their village but also in the county. Locally, a tithingman would have been elected annually (see Manorial Court extracts in Appendix A for later holders of this post). The tithingman was responsible for peace, although he became more responsible for local problems of a lesser degree at a later date.

Hooke Court

As mentioned in the previous chapter, Humphry Stafford had married Elizabeth Mautravers and came to the title of Hooke Court that way. In 1399 Stapleford still appears to have a manor as Humphry granted the moiety of 15 manors including Hooke and Stapleford to Geofrrey de Barnes and his wife Joan. Humphry Stafford's family came originally from Staffordshire and was a branch to which the Duke of Buckingham and Baron Stafford belonged.

Humphry Stafford rebuilt Hooke Court in stone in 1407 but the source of the stone is not clear. The house appears to have been L-shaped, perhaps limited by the moat. The north wing seems to have run alongside the moat. There were no architects in those days, so the stonemasons would carry out the building usually closely supervised by the person who was paying. The building would have been one room thick with each room inter-linking to the next. The 15th century wing was eventually demolished in 1965 having supposedly been left in poor repair by the Army, who used Hooke Court during the Second World War (although no record of this cause can be found!). The Stafford building was probably built on the foundations of the earlier house.

Taylor's map of Dorset, 2nd edition, shows Hooke Castle roughly on the site of the present

Hooke Court, a likely place for a market and fair, as mentioned in Hutchins.

St. Giles' Church

Elizabeth Stafford's will mentions the church of St. Giles, Stapleford suggesting that the current church may have been built 20 or 30 years after her death on the same site. This is one of the few pieces of evidence to give any possible location to Stapleford, but does conflict with other evidence.

The church is a Grade 1 listed building, dated as 15th century. The west arch of the church has a figure of a king on the South extreme and a bishop on the North. The crown of the king suggests that of Henry IV who reigned from 1399 to 1413, the head also having a large moustache, a characteristic of Henry IV. Assuming that this was Henry IV, it would suggest that the church was built about 1407 by the same builders as Hooke Court. Humphrey Stafford was patron by this time. Humphrey Stafford and his wife died within weeks of one another in 1413, so it is clear that it was built before 1413. In the north wall of the church, opposite the door is a recessed three light 15th century window with a carved bracket and canopy in its eastern reveal. This window may have been recessed to house an altar and shrine. If it was a shrine, to whom was it dedicated? The local saints were St. Juthware of Halstock and St. Whit of Whitchurch Canonicorum. There was also a Giles associated with Bridport! Next to it one sees an ornate 15th century niche with side-standards and a three-sided canopy with spire and pinnacles in which is the carved figure of St. Giles with his hind (this is more modern). Were these extravagant additions due to the later Sir Humphry?

The Royal Commission on Historic Monuments lists the following details of the church (comments in italics are the author's):

"Chancel 15th century east window (*the stained glass window is 20th century)*;
Vestry incorporates 15th century window and doorway;
Nave north wall 2 x 15th century window (east much restored);
south wall 16th century arch; south doorway 15th century;
west wall 15th century doorway;
south chapel early 16th century windows;
Bell 1563;
Brass north wall Edmund Semar 1523-4, the inscription reads

> "Of yor charyte pray for the soule of the late Edmund Semar late s'unt to Rob't Willoughby, knight, late Lord Broke, whiche Edmund deceased ye XIV day of January, the yer' of or Lord MDXXIV. On whose soul J'hu have mercy. Amen";

Font 15th century (*recent analysis suggests that the decoration on the rear stone work is more recent*);
Niches nave wall 15th century removed from south west angle of nave;
east splay of north west window bracket carved with angel holding skull 15th century;
Piscina in tower reset in west wall medieval;
Recess in chancel north wall 15th century."

The south aisle was probably added as a chantry chapel during this period by the later Sir Humphry Stafford to enable prayers to be said for him and his family.

When the swagger arch was cleaned in about 2001, the experts found some original paint on the 15th century window in the vestry (removed from somewhere else in the church in the 19th century), from the days when the church would have been highly decorated.

The relationship with Powerstock church mentioned in the last chapter continued to develop with more independence for Hooke. In 1437 Hooke gained parochial rights to burial; the only remaining right at that time not already granted. The vicar of Powerstock received two shillings each year for loss of income!

Roads and Communications

There was a medieval road from Evershot South to Hooke Court and North Poorton. It went along Yard Drove, a little south of Benville Bridge.

Individuals of Interest

In 1399 William Anger had an agreement with Humphrey de Stafford about the lands in the parishes of Houke, Stapleford, Overkentcombe, Netherkentcombe, ...Northporton, Southporton, Maydennyweton, Loscomb, etc. It appears that William had the right to all these lands, but granted them to Humphry, Elizabeth his wife and their heirs. We have no details of who William Anger was or why he had these rights and gave them to the Staffords.

In 1401 a similar problem arises with John Dynham, knight and his wife Matilda. They acknowledge that William was the legitimate owner. If they were to die without heirs the land will remain with the Staffords.

In 1405 the lady of the manor left money for Masses to be said in church for the repose of her soul after death. This money could have been used for the building of the south aisle or for the payment of a second priest for the chantry chapel (see later about her request at Abbotsbury).

John Stafford was the brilliant son of Sir Humphry Stafford, and he was born at Hooke Court. He was educated at Oxford and graduated as Doctor of Civil Law in 1413. In 1419 he became the Dean of the Court of Arches and Dean of Salisbury; in 1421 he was made Chancellor and Keeper of the Privy Seal; in 1422 he was treasurer and Dean at St. Martin's in London; by 1423 Dean of Wells. In 1424 he became Prebend of Stow-in-Lindsay, Lincolnshire and attached himself to Henry Beaufort, Bishop of Winchester. By 1425 his rapid rise continued as the Bishop of Bath and Wells. In 1281 the Council of Lambeth drew up a catechetical programme for the laity in Latin. In 1425 when John Stafford was Bishop of Bath and Wells, he had it translated into English and placed in every church in his diocese and required his archdeacons to provide copies for the clergy at not more than a 6d (pence) each.

In 1443 John Stafford became Archbishop of Canterbury. His experience made him indispensible and he retained his office of Chancellor. He tried to keep the peace between Suffolk and Gloucester (he had old political relations with the former). In 1450 he resigned the Chancery on the fall of Suffolk. He died in 1452. He was described as a "cautious, experienced official whose knowledge made him indispensible to government. He did little good, little harm". He had "high intellect, moral qualification, boundless hospitality". (He was reputed to be the father of a son by a nun!)

Another Sir Humphry Stafford became owner of Hooke Court. He was the son of the previous Humphry Stafford by his first marriage. Confusingly he also married an Elizabeth Mautravers, his stepsister, the daughter of Sir John Mautravers and the previous Elizabeth from her first marriage! He is the Humphrey Stafford "of the silver hand". Some texts suggest that he really did have a silver hand. It seems more likely that he was known for his generosity, perhaps for his own ultimate benefit!

In 1424 the new Humphry formed an agreement with Richard Loterigh of Toller Porcorum and Avicia his wife with regards to 20 acres of land, 1 messuage and one acre of meadow. Richard and Avicia acknowledge the tenements to be the right of Humphry but he gives them forty marks of silver.

Also in 1424: "Humfredus Stafford de Hoke in comitatu Dorsete miles tenet manerium de HOKE in predicto hundredo Ekerdon per servicium medietatus un f.m." (basically Humphry Stafford, a soldier, is acknowledged as holding Hooke in the Hundred of Eggardon).

In 1431 "Hundredum de Egerdon
De Humfredo Stafford pro dimidio feodo militis in Houk quod Robertus Syfrewast quondam tenuit..iij.s.iiijd" (identifying that he had to pay 3 shillings and 4 pence towards military costs as Robert Syfrewast had done).

In 1436 letters were passing to and fro in relation to the almshouse at Sherborne. One of the correspondents was Sir Humphry Stafford of Hooke. The Foundation Deed is engrossed on a six feet square piece of parchment and was signed by the five co-founders (The Bishop, Sir Humphry Stafford, Margaret Gough, Sir John Fountleroy, John Barrett) on 10th January 1437. "Sir Humphry Stafford, Knight, Lorde of Hooke, gave li in money and ix skes of timber towards the building". Richard Rochell's account for the "cost and purchase of wood" has some details of his excursions to Hooke. Rochell, the master, rode to Hooke to choose suitable oak trees, and carpenters were sent to mark and fell them. He set off from Sherborne on horseback with his friend John Dene, taking with him a present of apples and pears for Sir Humphry Stafford. They were going to inspect some oak trees with Sir Humphry's bailiff for the use of the new almshouse and Rochell makes mention in his account of fourpence he slipped into the bailiff's hand that day at parting! The accountant at Hooke and the carpenters at Stock (owned by Sir John Fountleroy) chose their trees well. The trees were from Hooke Woods (now called Hooke Park) for the building and in 1437 they were removed to the grounds of the abbey. The trees were stacked for seasoning in the churchyard at Sherborne for 6d. The oak in the almshouse chapel and hall today, shaped with adze, came in part if not wholly from the two woods of Hooke and Stock. The building was completed in 1445. The beams, crutches and screens in St. John's Almshouses today are still those oak beams from 1437!

Sherborne Abbey had a great fire in 1437. The rebuilding of the fan vaults incorporated 75 bosses in the whole vault. They are all of foliage design except for three heraldic shields in the centre of each bay, depicting the arms of Sir Humphry Stafford of Hooke. It is thought that he contributed to the rebuilding of the choir.

There are several documented statements about the Staffords in relation to Abbotsbury Abbey. For example after the Dissolution of the monasteries "St. Ann's Chapel built by Sir Humphry Stafford of Hooke (*N.B. spelling)* adjoining to St. Andrews". The "Ordination of the Strangeways Chapel" founded by Thomas Strangeways in 1505 identifies a tripartite indenture. One was Thomas Strangeways executor of Alianor, the late wife of Thomas who was one of the daughters of Walter Twynyho and Alice (daughter of Humphry Stafford of Hoke "with the silver hand").

An Instrument dated "ult. February 1505" requires a daily mass, the "Strangeways Mass", to be said for the souls of a long list that includes John Stafford, former Archbishop of Canterbury and Robert Willoughby, knt. late Lord Broke (he had become one of the joint owners of Hooke Court in 1469). Also in St. Mary's Chapel "6s. 8d yearly to a poor man, chosen by the Abbot according to an ordination of Humphry Stafford knt., founder of a mass called 'Staffords Mass', who shall be present at the daily mass of the said Humphry as well as the said Alianor."

The list of burials at Abbotsbury Abbey included "In 1405 Elizabeth, wife of Sir Humphry Stafford, knt snr. ordered her body to be buried in St. Andrew's Chapel, in the tomb of Sir John Matravers, knt. her former husband. In 1413 Sir Humphry Stafford the elder knt. in ditto. In 1442 Sir Humphry Stafford, Knt. in St. Anne's Chapel."

There are suggestions of funding for Cerne Abbey as well although these are alluded to rather than stated categorically. Clearly the Staffords had prayers being said for them in many places.

At some time another son, William Stafford, appears to have become the owner of Hooke Court. We know very little about him and he died in 1449, the new owner being the 10-year old William's son Humphry Stafford (not Sir Humphry this time) who married Isabel, daughter and heir to Sir John Bere. Humphry Stafford is a common name in the Stafford family, there are plenty of other Humphry Staffords!

He became Sir Humphry Stafford and was Sheriff of Dorset seven times. It is thought that it was he who changed the name of the river from Toller to Hooke (residents of Toller Whelme still insist on calling it the river Toller). The new Humphry Stafford (1439-1469) was very ambitious. It is probably this Humphry Stafford who was the one mentioned in the reign of Edward IV. In 1461 he succeed to the lands of his cousin Humphry(!), son of Sir John Stafford. He took up the Yorkist cause, fought in the Battle of Taunton in 1461 being knighted by the king, Edward IV, in the field. He became High Steward of the Duchy of Cornwall, Constable of Bristol, Keeper of Kingswood and Gillingham Forests (one source says: Warden or Constable of the Forest of Gillingham) and Joint Commissioner of Array in Dorset, Wiltshire and Somerset, all in 1461. He was created Baron Stafford of Southwick in 1464, became keeper of Dartmoor and Constable of Bridgwater Castle, both in 1464. In 1468 he was Commissioner to treat for peace with Francis Duke of Brittany. He was made a member of the Privy Council in 1469 and created Earl of Devon on May 7th that year (one source suggests by the murder of his cousin). He was denounced in the House of Commons on July 12th 1469 as "a caducious person whose covetous rule and gydynge". He was sent with 7000 archers to oppose Robin of Reasdale at Edgecote. He quarrelled with William Herbert, first Earl of Pembroke, and retired with all his troops; Pembroke was defeated. Edward IV ordered sheriffs to Devonshire and Somerset to put him to death. He was apprehended in Somerset and beheaded at Bridgwater on 17th August 1469 (just three months after becoming Earl of Devon). He left no heir.

The manor passed through the family on the female side: to the daughters of his aunt. Robert Willoughby, Lord Brooke, was the husband of one of those daughters and became the new owner of Hooke Court. Robert Willoughby died in 1522. His son died without leaving an heir and the estate passed to his two daughters by his second marriage. The eldest daughter was married to John Paulet, Marquis of Winchester, while the younger daughter married Charles Blount, eventually Lord Mountjoy. The latter title becoming extinct, the whole estate devolved to the Paulets. More of the Paulet family in the next chapter.

Interactions affecting people in the village

Changes in the Church and its impact on village life

As already stated, in 1437 the parishioners of Hooke used to bury their dead at Poorstock (Powerstock), and the burial fees went to the vicar of Poorstock. In that year they were given permission by the Bishop of Sarum to have their own graveyard. In compensation the vicar of Poorstock received a yearly pension of two shillings. It seems likely that Humphrey Stafford's influence enabled this change. Perhaps his generosity to the monasteries enabled Hooke to gain its own burial ground. Previously the parishioners would have had to pay to pass through the intermediate parishes of Toller Porcorum or North Poorton depending on the route.

Secular life

Vagabonds and vagrants were a problem. There were many attempts to stamp them out in the 16th century. However the harvest time in villages depended on all hands being available to ensure that this labour-intensive activity could take place as efficiently as possible.

The role of wives of farmers was not only to bring up the children but also to winnow the corn, make malt, wash and wring, make hay, shear corn, drive the plough, load the hay, ride to the market to sell butter, cheese, milk, eggs, chickens, not to mention keep the house clean and cook (she may have had one maid to help her if the income was sufficient). She was also in charge of the dairy and the account. It makes you wonder what her husband did!

Agriculture

Most of the land in Hooke at this time would have been pasture (land kept for grazing) and meadow (land kept to be mown for winter feed). The grassland involved human intervention, but would not have been the modern ploughing and planting of rye grass. The pasture (still prevalent in 1840 on the tithe map) would have been used for feeding stock for most of the year. In the winter the horses or oxen would be drawing the ploughs and working hard so good food was needed. The meadows provided the hay to be stored for the winter. The water meadows allowed stock to begin grazing earlier by keeping the frost off the ground. The land on Toller Down would have been rough and with gorse and other shrubs, so was suitable for the deer park. There is some evidence of the original plants in the area from the current plants found in the churchyard of St. Giles, some originating from the glacial era including Bird's-foot trefoil (that would now be found in meadows), buttercup, cuckoo-flower, self-heal and bugle (that would now be found in woodland grassland).

Sheep farming became popular in the 16th century. There were large increases in the number of sheep throughout the country. The increase in sheep and the reduction in other forms of agriculture caused a loss of jobs for farm labourers. Later in the century the price of wool fell and the price of wheat rose, so there was a tendency to plant wheat, although this was probably on the higher ground in Dorset. However, Dorset Poll and Dorset Horn sheep were generally useful animals. They were kept on the high ground on the chalk during the day and brought into the valleys at night to be kept in areas surrounded by hurdles (folds). The main purpose of the sheep was to fertilise the ground. Wool and meat were by-products. Perhaps the effect of falling wool prices had less impact in Dorset.

Textiles were a profitable industry. Not only were people knitting and generating garments for themselves but also trying to sell them. Fulling mills were a more efficient means of

generating wool cloth that was long lasting. There was such a mill in Hooke
have had this role since at least Domesday.

There were two agricultural fairs that seem to have occurred, one associated with Stapleford, the other on Toller Down, although this may have developed from the Stapleford Fair. The fairs would have provided entertainment as well as trade. The over-indulgence at these fairs by participants and some sharp practice by traders and entertainers kept the magistrates busy.

…arquis of Winchester, Dukes of Bolton up to …e Civil War (1460-1659)

…ackground and Village Structure

Nati… …ally

Nationally this period of history is eventful: the change to the Church of England (and back to Roman Catholicism and back again!); the discoveries of Canada and America that were to have such an impact in the future (particularly for agriculture) and the Civil War.

When the Boltons became the owners of Hooke Court, Henry VI only had one year of his first reign left, being replaced by Edward IV, a Yorkist, in 1461. Edward exhibited poor morals and his greed was inordinate. In 1470 Warwick succeeded in restoring Henry VI to a puppet throne, but Henry was killed in battle in 1471. Louis X restored Edward IV to England by the largesse of paying 75 000 crowns and an annuity of 20 000 crowns. In 1476 the Caxton press was set up and so began the era of printing. Richard III was king until 1485 and was killed in battle.

The first of the Tudors and Stuarts, Henry VII came to the throne in 1485 and married a Yorkist bringing to an end the War of the Roses. The struggle between the barons and the Crown ceased but taxes and fines had impoverished the nobles. It was the time of the merchant venturers and Cabot discovered Nova Scotia in Newfoundland and the navy was established. Henry's wife Elizabeth is to be found as the face of the queen on playing cards that were first invented in 1486. By 1509 Henry VIII had become king, the king who had six wives. He invaded France, the Scots invaded England, but were decisively beaten when King James IV and most of the Scots' nobility were slain. The Church in England became the Church of England at the same time as the rapid rise of the Protestant churches in Europe. The navy was separated from the army and Portsmouth naval dockyard came into existence. Edward VI became king in 1547 at the age of 9 and died when he was 16 in 1553. During his reign the Book of Common Prayer was printed in 1549, but the church was in chaos. Scotland and France formed an alliance and England went to war with Scotland. There were problems over pay particularly in the Norfolk Rising of 1549 because soldiers were unpaid. Lady Jane Grey became queen for 9 days in 1553, but was executed at the age of 17 to be followed by Mary who had had an appalling childhood. Mary married Phillip II of Spain but had no children. She attempted the wholesale conversion of England back to Roman Catholicism burning Bishops Latimer, and Ridley and Archbishop Cranmer at the stake. These years of turmoil in the church would have an impact on Hooke as will be elaborated later. The last of the Tudors was Elizabeth I (queen from 1558 – 1603). She was a remarkable woman noted for learning, sometimes wayward, often wise with a suggestion of an eye for the men. She re-instated her father's legislation for the church. After a variety of Roman Catholic plots she had Mary Queen of Scots executed in 1587. During Elizabeth's reign Virginia was founded, Drake circumnavigated the globe and it was a time of literary geniuses: Shakespeare, Sidney, Spencer, Bacon, Marlow to mention but a few. It seems unlikely that the literary works would have much effect in Hooke except perhaps at Hooke Court.

James I, the first Stuart, had a troubled reign. He considered himself to be king by Divine

Right, that he was above laws, but the House of Commons refused to pay his debts. He had ill-chosen corrupt favourites. In 1605 Roman Catholic sympathisers tried to blow up Parliament. The King James Bible was first printed in 1611.

The Puritans wanted tighter laws that were not forthcoming so in 1620 the Pilgrim Fathers sailed in the *Mayflower* to America. Charles I came to the throne in 1625; he had been a weak rickety child, but grew up courageous and high-minded. He had poor judgement, strong prejudices and was tactless. He also refused to accept dictation from Parliament. He carried out personal rule from 1629 – 1640, dissolving parliament and therefore had no money. The Civil War followed in which the King with nobility and peasants fought against Parliament and the middle classes; it was also a conflict of High Church against Puritans.

An account from South Perrott says that King Charles I spent the night at South Perrott on October 1st 1644. He had left Chard and kept to the road. He had dined with Lord Paulet (where? could it be Hooke?) and went to spend the night at South Perrott. The troops were 6 miles away at Evershot. The next day the troops moved to Kingcombe, while the king stayed at Maiden Newton. Both the king and the troops may have passed through Hooke if this story has any authenticity.

Later when attempting to regain the throne, King Charles II was in Dorset fleeing from the Parliamentary troops. He stayed at an inn in Charmouth because a ship was supposedly waiting for him and a boat would be sent to collect him. The boat did not arrive and he went on to Bridport but 1500 Puritan soldiers were also there so, after a hurried meal, he and his retinue went on the London road and turned inland, traditionally to Bradpole, but more probably into wooded areas around Powerstock, Hooke and Wraxall. After several hours, presumably following the ridge, they arrived at a small village inn in Broadwindsor. He eventually escaped to France.

Oliver Cromwell was a Puritan M. P. and a passionate orator. He had no military experience until the age of 44. In 1649 he was given command in Ireland and massacred garrisons at Drogheda and Wexford. He effectively became dictator in 1653. His son, Richard succeeded him but was not strong enough to settle a divided nation.

Village structure

By 1530 the monasteries had been destroyed and in many parts of the country the roads fell into disrepair as new owners took over the land but not the responsibilities. However, in theory, this should not have been a new problem in Hooke, although there is no evidence to suggest good or bad maintenance of the roads at this time. There was probably a road each side of the river from Toller Porcorum to Hooke, portions of which still exist as footpaths and others can be deduced from field boundaries. Road repairs became a statutory requirement enabling parish authorities to conscript labour for the purposes. Passenger-carrying vehicles began to appear as the first form of public transport. Whether the "coach" from Crewkerne to Beaminster and Maiden Newton existed at this time is not known.

The Church

Pevsner states that the interior of the church "has a great surprise - the entry arch from the nave to a former chantry or funeral chapel: a wide arch panelled and with lively leaf bands, a swagger display, by the shape of the chapel windows to be dated 1510 or 1520". The shield at the apex of the arch (Figure 5.1) bore the arms of Sir John Coleshill impaling those of his wife Elizabeth (Cheyney). Each side there would have been family shields all in glorious

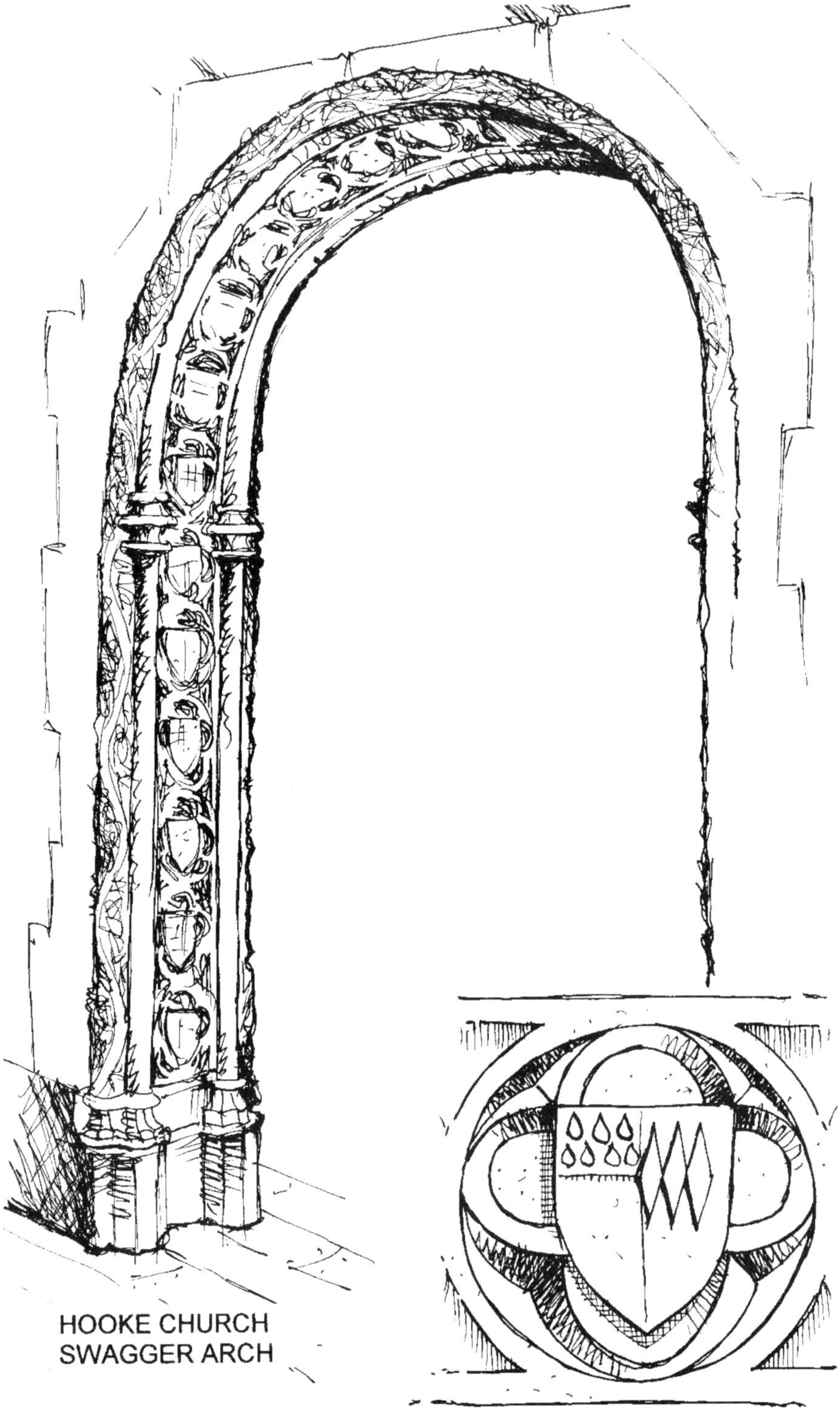

Figure 5.1 **The swagger arch in Hooke church with the apex coat of arms of Sir John Coleshill impaling those of his wife Elizabeth Cheney**

colour, no doubt defaced in Henry VIII's reign shortly afterwards. Such chantry or funeral chapels were included in churches from about the time of Henry VIII. If it was a chantry or funeral chapel, for whom was it built? It was called the "Lord's Aisle" in one document. The arch was built about 50 to 60 years after the last Hooke Stafford died, or was it there earlier and the arch is later? It seems to me that the windows in the South side are 15th century, suggesting that the arch was a later edition. At some time between 1510 and 1520 the swagger arch to the south aisle (probably the chantry chapel) was built. Was this a belated use of Elizabeth Stafford's money?

From 1520 to 1530 there may have been an expensive campaign to replace and renew statues and for re-ordering the chancel and high Altar. There may have been a new rood screen to ensure it competed with neighbouring parishes. Under the niche that currently has the more modern statue of St. Giles is an ancient brass dated 1523 in memory of Edmond Semor (the details of the inscription were given in the RCHM details about the church in the last chapter).

In 1542 the county of Dorset was transferred from the Diocese of Salisbury to the Diocese of Bristol. In 1552 The Dorset Commissioners for Edward VI give the following information about the Parish of Hooke "to the church's use there is appointed one Chalice. Sir John Style, parson there … Homfrey Wyllyams [Churchwarden]". The church is recorded as having had a tower with three bells in 1552. The current bell was cast in 1563. Its dimensions are diameter 36 inches, height 28.5 inches, inscription: HNT WP 1563 H.A.O.(?), the fourth letter is not clear. What happened to the old bells? Did the tower become unsafe? There was sometimes competition between villages to have the highest "tower", often meaning that a spire was placed on top of a tower unsuitable for the extra weight. Were the bells removed in accordance with the requirements of 1550? Did it collapse? Was the metal recast into a new bell? Such a re-cast may well have taken place within the village or the churchyard.

By 1550 the decorations on the arch, the elaborate robes of the priests and the stone altar at the east of the church would have all been removed along with any statues, paintings on the walls and any stained glass windows. There would have been a minister for the church. The south aisle of the church is thought to have been a chantry chapel. Previously it would have had a separate priest to say prayers for the deceased and the family (presumably the Staffords) although no specific records exist to support this argument. The second priest would no longer be there after the Reformation, causing problems for the Easter Communion, requiring a priest from another church to be called in to assist.

The church plate includes an Elizabethan chalice with paten cover (not unusual in Dorset). The cup is 6¾ in. in height: the sole mark on both pieces is on the cover with the date 1574. The shape is the usual Elizabethan style with a band of interlaced foliature round the bowl and ornamental moulding encircling the base.

In the 1580s there was a national campaign against the more extreme Puritans who considered each congregation a self-sufficient church of Christ. Dorset, in the area of Beaminster, had both dissident Roman Catholics and also separatist Puritans. It is likely that there would have been knowledge of these activities in Hooke, where the owner of Hooke Court was described as "blowing with the wind".

There was still plenty of potential for changes in the church. With James I coming from Scotland in 1603 there was much effort to remove the last vestiges of the Roman Catholic Church from the Church of England. It was expected that James, with his Presbyterian background, would support such moves. There were attempts to remove surplices, to have qualified clergy and many public debates were held. The symbol of the cross was considered by many to be idolatry. Whilst the effects on Hooke may have been limited, there was evidence of the Puritan effect with the citing of the rector for sedition (see later). The other extreme view saw the fine linen, and copes as symbols of the mystery of God, and that the Holy Bible should not be reduced to being available for direct access without the intercession of the priest. Bowing to the name of Jesus and treating the bread and wine as though they were the body and blood of Christ were central issues of the debate. Certainly the rector of Hooke by 1626 seemed to be more sympathetic to the Puritans than the William Lauds of the church (see later). It seems likely that practices were more focused on the word rather than the ritual. James's approach seemed to be to rid the church of both extremes and provide a large middle ground. The new Holy Bible (King James Version) was to become the basis and guide for a holy kingdom.

The interior of the church would have become very different. The church would have had a stark wooden table without a cloth in the chancel on the north wall. There would have been the Ten Commandments displayed on the wall. There would have been no images, no crucifixes. The proclaimed word of God was the focus. The Book of Common Prayer was about inclusion of the congregation. The new Holy Bible was clearly an essential part of this approach with its use of the English language expressing the beliefs of the 350 scholars and translators in wonderful glory. It was available in the church for anyone who could read, not only to be interpreted by a priest. It was the culmination of the many attempts to provide a Holy Bible in the vernacular. However there never was a single King James Version, as there are at least 24 000 variations because the book crept into the public arena without any registration, publication date or agreed text. No other bible was permitted to be printed from 1616 by order of the king. However the Geneva Bible continued to be printed until 1644! Only after the restoration of the monarchy did the bible become hallowed as having its origins before the great rupture. Its translation was created from the social structures of the time of rigid hierarchies, subservience and power with glory – the origins of much of the wonderful language that is used.

By the 17th century there would have been another alteration to the church, the altar would have re-appeared on the east wall with altar rails.

Hooke Court

The Humphry Stafford that was beheaded had no issue, so his aunts' daughters, Elizabeth and Alianor, and a nephew, Sir Robert Willoughby, became heirs before 1485. Elizabeth married John Coleshill (whose marriage is celebrated with the swagger arch in the church) and Alianor married Sir Thomas Strangways. Elizabeth died leaving no heir. The estate was divided and John Willoughby became Lord of Hooke, left it to his son who became Lord Brooke, having descended from the Pawlitts in Wiltshire. His son, Robert succeeded him. Robert's son by his first wife died; his daughters by his second marriage (this wife being daughter of Thomas, Marquis of Dorset), married John Paulet, Marquis of Winchester and Charles Blount, eventually Lord Mountjoy. Hooke became jointly owned by the Blounts and the Pawlitts (Paulets) on the death of Robert Willoughby in 1522. In the early 17th century (1609) the manor devolved to the Paulets when a Charles Blount died without heirs. The Marquis of Winchester became the sole owner of Hooke.

Humphry Stafford, according to Coker (referred to in Hutchins 1861 Volume 2, Pg 182) built the house early in the fifteenth century (there are various dates, but it would seem to be about 1408). William Paulet, Marquis of Winchester, probably developed the west wing after acquiring the manor in 1609. John Paulet, Marquis of Winchester, played a major part in many local battles, appearing to be a senior officer for the Royalists. The tenant was Henry Samways. Details of the house are in RCHM documents and there are some photographs in the Dorset County Museum from the time before the 15th century north wing was destroyed.

One source suggests that in 1646 the decaying house of the Marquis of Winchester, Hooke Court, was stormed and burnt to the ground. Parliamentary soldiers burned the house and Samways was later compensated for the loss of goods for more than 60 pounds. In March 1646 Richard Conway was ordered to fell, sell and dispose of all timber fit to be felled for the benefit of the state. Perhaps this would also include Westcombe and Ridge Coppices, the sources for the deer pales, which presumably fell into disrepair. In 1647 10s was paid to a mason to dig for lead amongst the ruins. He was so successful that he found 15 hundredweight of lead! A receipt dated July 5 acknowledges £5 for 15 cwt. of burnt lead at Hooke. Evidence of the fire was seen when the building was destroyed in 1965.

The manor was sequestered and sold by Cromwell to Thomas Jarboys. The Minterne family became tenants of the house and were given responsibility by the Dorset Standing Committee for collecting rents and fines and maintaining the mansion house to prevent further ruin. With the restoration of the monarchy the Marquis of Winchester regained the manor and repair work was carried out. He also held Powerstock.

The Role of Magistrates

In 1588 the Armada was expected and the magistrates supervised the stores of pikes for use against the Armada. Local 'volunteers' were expected to take part in repelling any invasion.

In London there were regular outbreaks of the plague: 1592, 1603, 1625, 1636 and then the great outbreak of 1664. Not everyone caught the plague, it seems that some may have had a natural immunity their blood being unattractive to fleas. The last recorded case was in 1679 in Rotherhithe. Bridport was affected by plague in 1625. The next round of the plague started in London in 1636. In January 1637 Agnes Hoble of Toller Porcorum was infected by her late husband with a 'dangerous and deadly disease whereof he dyed and wherein she so languisheth'. The magistrates were required to help people that were affected. In this case they required £12 to be raised to help (with a cure?) and anyone who did not contribute as requested would have goods 'distrained'. It seems likely with a case so near that Hooke could have been affected, but there is no clear evidence to support the supposition.

Buildings in Dorset

Cob Cottages were common buildings in Dorset by about the middle of the seventeenth century (Figure 5.2). The chalk was mixed with clay and straw used to bind the mixture together. Walling was built up in layers of 2' – 3' high and 2' thickness, each layer being left to settle for a day or two before another was added.

It was a laborious process used for buildings of humble status. The typical plan of such houses was one or two rooms and few had storage space, larders or sculleries. The bake-oven was generally built into the wall beside the fireplace. A brick or plaster hood was cantilevered out over the hearth; this was rather unstable and was gradually replaced by bringing the whole chimney forward. Occasionally stone seats were hollowed out of the walls on either side of the fireplace. The early cottage staircase was a steep ladder, but a compact staircase built around a newel or pillar in a corner by the chimney replaced this. Many floors were plastered by packing clay on wattle laid over joists, while red bricks, tiles or stone flags were used for the ground floor although mud seems to be more likely in poor Hooke. The thatched cottages shown in the photograph of Hooke church in 1870 may be remnants of this type of cottage.

The cottages called Brook Cottages and St. Francis Cottage are reputed to have been built during Cromwell's time. They both have chalk blocks in their construction, being the only houses in Hooke of that construction. Tradition suggests that the chalk blocks were brought from Sherborne when the castle was ransacked, although there is no evidence to support this romantic idea! Both houses were of lower construction in the past, St. Francis Cottage still having roof beams upstairs from the previous roof. The lower level of the roof of Brook Cottages can be seen on the gable end.

Figure 5.2 **Artist's impression of the inside of a cob cottage.**

Individuals of Interest

The social hierarchy in the late 15th century was:

Laity	Clergy
Dukes Earls Barons	Archbishops Bishops Abbots
Knights Esquires Gentlemen	Rectors Vicars
Yeomen Husbandmen Labourers	Lesser Clergy
Servants Marginals	

Hooke had a peculiar hierarchy with dukes, gentlemen, rectors then labourers, servants and marginals. Yeomen appear later in the manorial court records.

George Penne had acquired the lease of Toller Whelme from the Paulets in 1623 and bought the estate outright in 1630. He was a Roman Catholic and his family had married into wealthy land owning families. He was the son of Anne Stroud of Parnham who had married Giles Penne. George died in 1640 and left the estate to his namesake, a nephew, George Penne. The new George Penne was an ardent and politically motivated Catholic who was one of four Dorset collectors of Catholic subscriptions gathered to support Charles I on his Scottish campaign. In 1644 Prince Maurice's Royalist troops are reported to have started a major fire in Beaminster. In 1648 George Penne provided trees from Chedington and Hooke for the re-building of Beaminster after the fire. It is not clear what Penne's relationship with Hooke was, although clearly he either leased some land or possibly even owned it. The Deer Park was listed as Penne's Field on one map.

The Montagu family was making itself part of the elite of the country about this time. Lord Montagu was an important part of Cromwell's hierarchy and continued to succeed under Charles II whom he was partly instrumental in getting back to England. He was one of many appalled by the disorder that occurred after the death of Cromwell. He was also made Earl of Sandwich probably because of his naval successes (and Viscount Hinchinbrooke, the name of the family home). The sandwich is named after a later member of the family who was a great gambler and wanted to eat his meat whilst gambling so had it wrapped in bread. The Montagu family became part owners of the Hooke estate in the 19th century.

The Paulets came from a Somerset place of that name. The first Paulet to be ennobled Marquis of Winchester was a favourite of Henry VII. He changed "to Henry VIII religion", was described as a court sycophant and timeserver. He became a protestant under Edward VI, a papist under Mary sending Protestants to be burned at Smithfield and returned to being a protestant under Elizabeth persecuting, fining, mulcting and putting to death papists. He became Marquis of Winchester in Edward VI reign. He was Lord Treasurer under Mary and Elizabeth! He managed to retain office for three reigns by "being a willow not an oak"! The Paulet family was of Basing, Hants and Hooke Manor, Dorset. The Marquis died in 1572.

"William Paulet, Marquis of Winchester augmented the new buildings at Hook Court and often lived there, but his successors have not thought so well of it, wherefore it is like to run to decay". In Hooke Court is a late perpendicular chimneypiece with a deep lintel carved with sub-cusp quatrefoils, the centre bearing the Paulet arms that must have been brought in, because the Paulets came to Hooke in only 1609. This was the 5th Marquis whose house was stormed at Basing by the Roundheads after withstanding the siege for four years.

The Mundens of Coltleigh

There seemed to be some connection between the Marquis and John Munden of Coltleigh. Coltleigh is described as "the land sprung upwards towards the north east, ending in the rough crest of Coltleigh Hill, at times raked by gales, at times muffled in mist as in a white woollen wrap … and below them the farmhouse of Coltleigh, with fields sprawling beyond it with an open-handed splendour till they met the trees of Hooke Park". The farmhouse is still there and the fields sprawling beyond. The trees of Hooke Park still provide the boundary, suggesting that the deer park had already moved to this new venue. Was it there in 1572 when this was stated? The venue seems to conflict with other evidence. John Munden was a Catholic. It is most likely that the young Munden was influenced during the early sixties by a lively intelligence abroad in Dorset. Thomas Harding, a Fellow of New College and Prebendary and Treasurer of Salisbury Cathedral, had been deprived for refusing to take the Oath of Supremacy and ordered to remain within sixteen miles of Monkton Farleigh in Wiltshire, where the bishop of Salisbury had certain rights in the manor house and within twenty miles of Toller Whelme in Dorset. Toller Whelme, in the parish of Corscombe, was the Harding's family house and was within easy walking distance of Coltleigh, lying in the secluded valley that led to Hooke, the great house owned by the Marquis of Winchester. The old Marquis was pliant in his religious principles, bending with the prevailing wind, and his sons were Catholic: Thomas Paulet of Melplash Court and Eleanor his wife were later cited as recusants at Netherbury. The Munden family were in danger several times during this century. They seem to have been given assistance by the Marquis in avoiding detection.

The Minternes

The Minterne table tomb by the south wall of the church has the inscription "Here lyeth the body of Henry Minterne Gent of Hooke who deceased 9th day of January AODi 1651…." The inscription goes on to suggest that others are also buried there. Such a table tomb in Oxfordshire would have a crypt underneath. The final Mintern (the final 'e' seems to have been dropped) connection is in 1920s when the Mintern Trust was set up on the death of a member of the family who had emigrated from England to Australia. The trust was for the help of the poor of the village and is still in existence.

A Rector in trouble through a Minterne

The rector of Hooke in 1626 was Mr Nicholas Day. He preached a sermon before Christmas that year and it would appear that he was a Puritan. He would certainly have found himself at variance with many of his parishioners who were tenants of the Marquis of Winchester. Three men from the parish: Robert Sprage, William Webber and Henry Minterne (called young Mr Minterne, son of the farmer of Hooke Manor) were prosecution witnesses for a court case of sedition brought against the rector. It would appear that young Mr Minterne was taking notes during the sermon (so here was a farmer's son in 1626 who had been educated). The rector saw that notes were being taken and said " Write on, Mr Minterne, write on I feare thee not but would speake so much though the Kinge were in presence". The prosecution suggested that the rector had complained that the land was governed not by justice but by bribery “Kinges could not contain themselves in their oone Kingemdoms and that they seeke to make invasion of other countrys and to sack their goods … illtreat their women … and commit all other villany what not which makes all nacons say ‘Is this the fruit of Religion?’ which God is not well pleased with and that the effect shewith itt selfe by the late Repulse and how the waters be cleere when the fountains are infected.” The “late repulse” presumably referred to the failure of Lord Wimbledon’s attack on Cadiz. Mr Day defended himself and explained that he was expressing the enormous cruelty the Spaniards used towards the Indians when referring to sacking of goods and the ill treatment of women. His comments about extortion and bribery were the words of the Prophet Isaiah about the lands of Judah and Israel. He was committed to the Assizes, but the consequences do not appear to have been serious because he held the living until 1640 (from 1593)!

Interactions affecting people in the village

Changes in the Church and its impact on village life

If we think that we live in times of great change, it is probably nothing to the turmoil of 50 years or so during this period. All the structure of social life was devastated from 1530. What follows are the likely changes at Hooke based on the known effects in the diocese of Exeter and Salisbury. Hooke was in the diocese of Bristol, but it seems unlikely that there would be any significant difference. The impact on the life of villages was dramatic, changing nearly all the social structure, the roles of individuals and the yearly sequence of events.

If there were any seats in the church, these would be for the elderly and infirm. The women and men were on opposite sides of the church. In 1520 there would still have been several altars in the church. One would have been to a local saint, possibly St. Whit as at Whitchurch Canonicorum. The church would be densely peopled with saints whose images filled the building. Canon law required that either side of the high altar were the principal statue of the Virgin and the patronal image (St. Giles) each in decorated niches (probably like those remaining opposite the South door). Weekday masses would be at a side altar where there was an image of Jesus possibly holding a globe, the Salvator Mundi. This side altar could have been in the niche of the window in the north wall opposite the entrance to the church. Usually included in village churches were either St. Loy or St. Eilgius patron saint of smiths and carters (usually portrayed holding a horseshoe, hammer and horse’s leg), as well as St. Anthony, healer of men and farm animals, St. Anne (to enable barren women to have children). Each saint would have had candles for the altar and their own store, probably the responsibility of a group of people in the village (in some villages there would be Guilds, each with their own uniform). There would be sets of clothes, shoes, and jewellery for each saint’s statue. Each saint’s fund had a warden who could be male or female and there were two chief wardens (there could be as many as 12 wardens). Anyone unwilling to become a warden was fined providing more money for the store.

In Morebath in Devon a flock of sheep supplied the income from the wool and the lambs for an altar. Other people would keep bees for the church to provide the wax for the candles. There would be a chandler in the village who provided the Great Paschal taper. There was not only a heavy involvement from the village socially but also economically. People gave clothes, rosaries etc. to adorn the statues. The church house (ale house) would hold events such as a visiting musician and all would be expected to attend, having paid, and also to drink the ales to provide more income (modern social functions in Hooke for the church bear a remarkable similarity!). A small group of up to four usually provided financial security and provided funds that were claimed back as they could be paid. The lord of the manor would probably be one of these financiers.

There would be a parish clerk. He prepared the vestments, vessels, books, lights (candles) and altars for services. He assisted with the liturgy, saying or singing responses, reading the epistle at mass. He also locked the church half an hour after the end of the last service. He was chosen by the priest and paid for by all. The payments were often in kind providing problems if there was a poor crop. He also carried and distributed holy water around the parish, repelling evil and bringing blessing, also curing animals. Not only would there be Mass but also Matins, First and Second Vespers (Evensong).

Much of village life centred on the main feasts of the church with much active participation, all of which was to be abandoned. Some examples of the importance of the church with its festivals and activities to the village are given in the following paragraphs.

The church would have had many wall paintings, images of several saints, an octagonal font (still there at the west end, although two of the carvings at the rear appear to be more modern). The raising of the Host would be the high point of Mass, but communion was not received by the laity (except at Easter). Those members of the congregation that could read would have primers. The rich would have their own chapel, for example the chantry chapel (probably the origin of the South aisle of the church) and their own priest.

The rood screen in the church would have an image of Christ on the cross, St. John and the Virgin Mary. There was powerful imagery at feasts such as Candlemas and Presentation of Christ in the Temple. Parishioners were required to present 1d (old pence) and a candle to the priest at Mass. Candles were often burned in front of the principal image of the Virgin in the church. There would be a blessing of candles and a procession before Mass. The procession would include actors who would go through the village first. In Lent the crucifix would be covered with a large painted veil.

Holy Week ceremonies were elaborate (perhaps as seen in Spain today). On Palm Sunday the shrine of the local saint would be sheltered with a silk canopy and carried out into the churchyard. Many of the village would be dressed up as Old Testament prophets in this procession. After Mass on Maundy Thursday all the altars would be washed with water and wine. The stripping of the altars represented a stripping of Jesus for death. On Good Friday there would be preaching but no Mass. The veiled crucifix would be brought into the church with solemn and penitential celebration. It was wrapped in linen cloths and placed in a timber sepulchre (or a hollowed out space) in the north side of the chancel of the church. The Priest's gestures and movements would recall memories of Maundy Thursday and Good Friday. On Easter morning the cross was carried in procession and placed on an altar on the north side of the church. The empty sepulchre was a focus of attention in Easter week. There may have only be an *annual* receiving of Communion by the villagers on Easter Sunday. For feast days there would be a high mass that required a second priest or deacon. With a chantry chapel at Hooke this would not be a problem. During the weeks preceding Easter the parish priest would spend hours hearing the whole parish's confessions.

The use of processions, acted scenes and images all contributed to the imaginative powers of the villagers. Private meditation would involve vivid mental pictures of Christ especially on the cross (as on the rood screen). Confession was essential. There was probably a specific shrine related to the church that was possibly opposite the South door where there is a recess in the wall.

The fabric and furnishing of the church involved a large investment by the laity. The raising of funds was as much a necessity then as now. There would be a large list of books, robes, vestments, cups, plates etc., bells, images, bier, etc. The whole was a collective responsibility. By the time that the current church was built it would have been well equipped either with new or old materials passed on from its two predecessors. There may have been groups (or Guilds) responsible for providing the clothes, candles, etc for a particular altar. The funds could become a major feature of the village economy. As already stated a Guild may even have a sort of uniform, even if it was only a hood of a particular colour. It would have an annual subscription. Immoral behaviour could result in expulsion from the Guild. If a member of a Guild died, all the other members were expected to attend the funeral

The beating of the bounds at Rogationtide would be an annual event to drive evil spirits out of the community. Eating and drinking (at the church alehouse that was probably alongside or near to the church) would usually follow, again enhancing community spirit. Religion was the significant focus of social life.

The liturgical calendar was the only calendar and it was enshrined in law. Parishioners were expected to fast for 40 days in Lent and employers were expected to adhere to the 40-50 feast days each year (that meant 40–50 days of holiday for the villagers). The church gave the poor some relief from their distress. On many saints' days there would be a procession through the village. At the end of the processions there would sometimes be bonfires and communal drinking. There would also be dramas based on miracles and saints' lives often with banners with words printed. Saints were perceived as friends and helpers, the patron saint could be relied on ex-officio to care for his parishioners. New saints meant new shrines, so churches were often filled with statues. Female virgin saints who had usually been viciously and physically damaged were popular: Saint Katherine, Saint Margaret, and Saint Barbara.

Using a metal detector a 15th century gold ring was found in a field near to Hooke Park. The ring shows four female saints each with a building in their hands; three of these saints are probably Katherine, Margaret and Barbara. The ring is held by the Dorset County Museum. The ring could have been used as a sign for a person to be recognised or could have just fallen off somebody's finger.

Other village activities would be at Lammastide at the beginning of August when the churchyard was tidied and cleaned.

The reeve or churchwarden controlled behaviour. There would have been lists of demeanours that were not acceptable.

In 1471 pestilence was rife in the West Country. There would have been pilgrimages to holy places: Whitchurch Canonicorum was perhaps the nearest shrine with the remains of a saint.

Children often died very young and were called "creature". The child was usually christened when the head appeared and the same name would be used for more than one member of the family. From 1536 parishes had been required to give basic reading and religious instruction to all children. The parson usually provided the lessons. The lesson would often be given in church. In other villages such as Salway Ash there was a Dame School, but there is no evidence of one in Hooke. There is no documentary evidence of any educational provision in Hooke. Being a poor agricultural village it is possible that children were expected to work and the lord of the manor may not have insisted on the requirement being carried out.

The sudden changes that occurred during this period were very dramatic for the whole of the village life. Although they may not have been so dramatic in Hooke, nevertheless the traditional images were attacked, relics and miracles were forbidden, as were pilgrimages. Saints' days were swept away (including St. Giles) causing a large loss of holidays for the poor and the cult of the Virgin Mary was reduced. No candles were permitted before any images. In 1535 priests were to teach abolition of "the abuses of the Bishop of Rome, his authority and jurisdiction and commanded to teach the Royal Supremacy". In 1536 all holy days within law terms or harvest period from the beginning of July were abolished, the remainder were damaging to the country's economy according to Cromwell. In 1538 the Bishop of Salisbury, Nicholas Shaxton ordered no decking of images with gold or silver, no kneeling to images, no oats, wool, cakes etc, to be offered. A similar order occurred in many diocese. Bibles were to be paid for from funds for saints. All relics were to be sent to the bishop, although many were buried or hidden. It was also suggested the Rogation should be abolished. All parents, employers were required to catechise children and servants using the Lord's Prayer, Creed, and Ten Commandments in English rather than Latin. There was a general attack on the cult of pilgrimage and images.

There was fierce debate about church reforms, probably often taking place in the church alehouse. If there was such an alehouse at Hooke it was probably in the grounds of the present church, perhaps where the cottage was to the west. "Church reforms represented problems to the villages of Somerset and Dorset. Church reform was promoted within the parishes by a few active supporters, while the majority of clergy and parishioners wisely avoided expressing any opinion." Criticism of the parish priest was rife, such as in Somerset: "He will noe wyse declare unto his said parishioners the word of god according to his dewtye and as hee is bound to doo, but utterly dispyseth and is redy to undo all those that are gladde and willing to have the Scripture and god's word set forth and preched unto them and also rede it themselves, and calleth them heretycks." There was considerable resistance by the clergy to the scriptures being available to the congregation. There was a requirement in 1538 to have Coverdale's 'Great Bible set up in some convenient place'. It was only in 1537 that Tyndale was executed for his work in translating much of the bible into English! However preaching was not generally considered important.

From 1538 there should be one bible set up in Church and a register kept of all weddings, christenings and burials. The register was to be kept in a safe place. The church coffers were to be kept with two locks and two keys, one held by the priest and the other by the churchwardens. Once a quarter the priest was to preach that no trust should be placed in statues. The focus was to be charity, mercy and faith as prescribed in scriptures.

By 1540 far fewer parishioners shouldered any responsibility. There were now only 6 elected wardens. There were fewer chores and fewer opportunities for influence. In 1543 inland parishes such as Hooke paid towards coastal defences and maintaining a fire beacon. A significant part of the parish income now went to the king. In December 1545 the king needed money, so the first Chantry Act confiscated maladministered funds, priests were pensioned off and the capital was retained to fund the war. It may be that the end of the chantry at Hooke occurred at this time. By 1547 the rosary was rejected totally as was praying on beads. All processions were forbidden; banners and streamers were redundant. Only two lights (candles) were permitted on the high altar, no others. Commissioners were sent to ensure that all this had been implemented. Something had to be sold to pay for the visitation! There was an order to cease keeping church ales. So there was a calamitous loss of income. All the property of guilds, lamps, chantries, etc was to cease. Holy Communion was instituted in 1547/8. All of the congregation were to receive communion in the form of bread and wine often, not just at Easter. An inventory of all church goods was required. Many of the statues, their attributes, the altar cloths, and vestments were sold. The church ale-house now had no use and would probably have been let off. The Book of Common Prayer was required as from January 1549. Holy water distribution was abolished. Confirmation could take place when the young people were old enough to memorise and read the catechism.

Further changes that would have affected the already demoralized villagers occurred. All walls were to be whited. Catholic books were to be destroyed. There were to be no altars, saints were removed from niches, only one bell could be used to call for a service. Inventories were required from 1552. In 1553 Edward VI confiscated church copes and all but a single small bell were to be removed from towers. In 1550 there were three bells in Hooke. By 1563 there was one bell – was the tower pulled down? Was the bell recast in the church grounds from the previous bells? All males over 14 were required to take an oath accepting the provisions of the Act of Supremacy with Royal Commissioners appointed in each county. All church valuables were confiscated except the minimum for reformed rites.

Suddenly, however, all seemed to be going back to the former times. By 1554 Mary had become Queen and much was to be re-instated. Bibles were collected up from churches. The power of the word was to be replaced by the power of the ritual and symbolic. Every church was required to have a basic set of frontals, vestments, cope, etc. The costs of re-instating these requirements to a poor village like Hooke must have been devastating. Most churches were in dire need of repair by the end of the century. Perhaps Hooke was lucky because its church was well built and relatively new. Clergy were now required to be celibate (about 15% were married!). Mass books were loaned for 2/-. Ceremonies and the Easter sepulchre were restored (often dug up from where it had been buried). By 1553/4 there was to be only one warden.

An end to the changes had not occurred yet. In 1558 Elizabeth became queen. The Book of Common Prayer was re-introduced from Whit Sunday, June 9th. It was available as a paper back at 2s and in hard covers at 3s 4d. The abolition of images of all sorts, including stained glass windows followed. There was a rigorous suppression of the externals of Catholicism. Documentary evidence had to be shown that all these requirements had been carried out with the names of the wardens and the names of the purchasers when anything was sold. Visitations occurred to check that the orders had been carried out. The rood loft was to be removed. There was excommunication for not complying. It took about 20 years for the full effect. A whole basis of village life was stamped out finally.

At this time the clergy did not give sermons and many could not even read. Some clergy were accused of forgetting that the church was a house of prayer and allowing it to become a house of "talking, walking, brawling, minstrelry, hawks and dogs". The clergy were often very poor. However by the end of the century the educational standards had improved and their social standing had been enhanced. Stipends had increased; many clergy had families (marrying had been allowed again by Elizabeth since 1547), so the increase in stipend was often necessary to support the family. The parsonage was becoming a more comfortable house and the clergy were gaining a similar status to the local squire.

Impact of the Civil War

The Tudor monarchs overthrew the Catholic Church, set up Protestantism, restored Catholicism, and then settled for the compromise under Elizabeth, leaving a legacy of hatred for Catholics and many Protestant sects, such as Puritans who disliked the established church with its bishops and tithes. The Puritans became political opponents of the king. The

Civil War (1642) was brought about by the king's (Charles I) refusal to accept restrictions from Parliament, which in turn refused to accept his supremacy. The war split the nation, dividing families and enhanced rifts in the church. Within seven years there were no kings, lords or bishops. Although these reforms were reversed, the elected House of Commons was an essential part of the government from then onwards. Religious ceremonies for marriages were declared invalid in August 1653, civil ceremonies could take place in church presided over by senior administrative figures. What happened in a village like Hooke is not clear with Hooke Court having been bought by Thomas Jarboys. Did he act as local magistrate at that time?

The labourers were often unaware of the Civil War. It does seem likely that in a small village like Hooke they would have noticed the change in owner and asked why? The Civil War seemed to do little to relieve poverty. Labouring people and out-servants earned about £15 a year per family; cottagers and paupers struggled on £6 10s per family. It may have been even less in Dorset! Any poor people unable to support themselves were to be sent back to the parish where they were last settled. Parish constables ensured these returns and were an expensive item on landowners. The welfare policies of the early 17th century were based on the statutes of 1598 and 1601. The three principles were: 1) the deserving poor who were provided for from parish taxation in cash or kind: the overseer had discretion based on moral rather than economic grounds; 2) the undeserving idle who were the ones described above that were to be returned to their own parish by the parish constables through other parishes where the constable took similar action; 3) the unemployed/labouring poor wishing to work who were seen as deserving but able, and the parish overseer would provide hemp and flax on which to work and the profit going back to the parish. Much of this legislation derived from the poor harvests from 1594 – 1597 when a large number were starving to death and the stealing of foodstuffs soared. By the middle of the 17th century there were compulsory poor rates in nearly all parishes from 1640. There were further harvest failures for 1647 - 1650. The poor rates continued from the 1690s until 1834.

Local medicine and witchcraft

In the mid-17th century, during the time of the Long Parliament, there was severe punishment of witchcraft. There were many who provided protection against pain and death. All manner of treatments were given and the local witch may well have been the main source of medicine from herbs. Such a person or people seem to have been likely in a rural area such as Hooke. There were almost hysterical witch-hunts. There was a notable case at Exeter when three witches were convicted on the flimsiest evidence.

The Role of Women

There was also conflict between the sexually liberated low life in cities and the ideal of continence and perpetual wrestling with temptation of the Puritans. It is not clear how the two cultures stood in Hooke, but it is likely that there were some difficulties because the surrounding area contained Catholics, Puritans and strong Non-conformists.

The business of the Hundred and the magistrate's court

The business of the Hundred was transacted at Hooke Court still protected by its moat. The Marquis acted as local judge/magistrate. An interesting case was brought before him in 1582. John Meer of Abbotsbury was something of a madman having persuaded himself that he had a mission from God to torment and plague men of this world. It was said of him in 1584 "he had slandered the most part of the knights, magistrates and best appointed gentlemen in the county of Dorset". In 1582 he had been accused by a neighbouring Justice, George Tilley of Poyntington of "a suspicion of felony" before the Marquis of Winchester in his house at Hooke, and the case was referred to the Quarter Sessions at Bridport. Meere revenged himself by seducing Tilley's daughter.

Middle class funerals

Any funerals of those related to the owners of Hooke Court or the middle classes in Hooke would probably have taken place at night, as this was the fashion probably brought by the Marquis of Winchester from Basing to Hooke.

Agriculture

Hooke Park

The bailliff's accounts for 1510-1511 records an income of £4 12s 6d for agistments, in other words for grazing cattle. The deer park is described "in a compass one mile or thereabouts" (S P Dom 1583) one of the few Dorset deer parks that still contained deer (others were: Gillingham, Holt, Melbury, Melcombe and Sherborne). Leland stated "Hoke Park, having an ancient manor Place in it, but a mile by East South East from Beaminster". It is interesting that he saw the Manor House as being in the park, did it have a larger area than we think, or was it Leland writing from brief notes? Certainly deer for food was the purpose of the park.

The park (Figure 5.3), was surveyed for Elizabeth I in 1583 for the purposes of breeding horses for the army. The record of Dorset parks identifies one park in the hundred of Eggardon called "Hooke Parke which is the land of the right honourable the Lord Marquis of Winchester containing in compass one myle or thereabouts and his occupation in which the parke there is as well as deere kept also mares according to the statute." A deer pale surrounded the park. The pale consisted of: a ditch about 4 feet deep, a bank outside that about 4 feet high surmounted by either a hedge or oak palings. The latter seems likely, in this case, because there are oak coppices on two sides of the park. Unfortunately a new owner had the land ploughed over the last of the ditches in Spring 2000 at the north side of Westcombe Coppice.

John Speed's map shows it as one of a dozen deer parks in Dorset. The maps of Speed and Saxton clearly show the park north of the village. "There, a mile up the valley stream, still issues from a pond which is still called 'Park Pond' and all around are field names such as 'Park Mead', 'Park Bottom', 'Park Cowlease'". The great pond in Hooke Park (presumably Park Pond) was identified as a source of the river by Coker/Gerard. The name of the village is given as Hooke or Oake (perhaps the mistaken presumption that it originated from the name of the tree?).

Leland also states that "The most common opinion is, that Frome riseth in a great pond in Hooke Park …" . (Gerard later discusses the various streams that flow down through the Tollers to Maiden Newton "the first of them issueth out of a great pond in Hooke Park…). Not statements that the residents of Toller Whelme would uphold (whelme=source!), so the river from Toller Whelme to Hooke is still called the river Toller by the residents of Toller Whelme.

During the Civil War the deer park seems to have come into disrepair. Presumably the deer escaped. Some time after the restoration of the Monarchy the Marquis of Winchester had Hooke returned to his ownership. It seems that the deer park was moved to nearer to the manor house, but not necessarily the current Hooke Park.

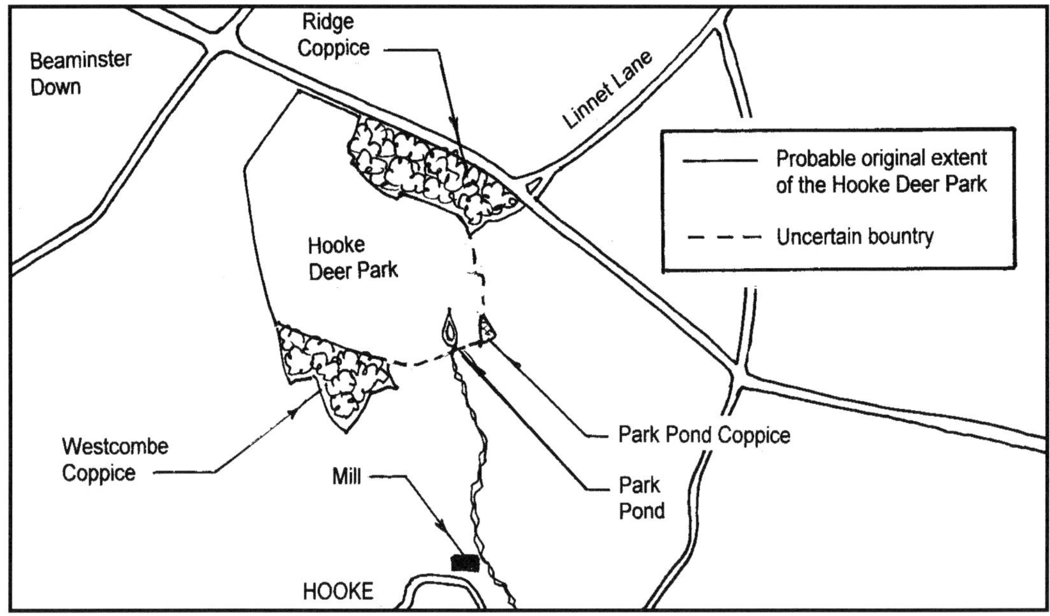

Figure 5.3 **Hooke Medieval Deer Park** (after Cantor and Wilson)

Use of woodland

As identified earlier on the chapter, in 1648 George Penne provided timber trees now standing at Chedington and Hooke to the value of £500 to be designated for use. (This was for the repairs to Beaminster after the first fire involving Prince Maurice's troops). Woodland at this time had two uses: timber and wood. Timber was used for buildings and wood for fires. The timber trees would be a minority and the underwood the majority. The timber would provide beams and planks. Coppicing, probably on a five-year cycle, and the branches of felled timber trees produced the wood. Seedlings would replace the timber trees. The wood would provide rods, poles, and logs and be used for fencing and wattlework, but the bulk would be firewood. The timber trees would almost certainly be oak.

At this time underwood was the more important and renewable product. Underwood would consist of hawthorn, hazel, blackthorn in this area. In the two coppices to the north (Westcombe and Ridge) the oak may well have been coppiced for the deer palings at the top of the banks. The length of the park boundary was about 3-4 miles. The coppicing would be on a 30-year cycle. Boundaries were often a great fence and a ditch to prevent deer from damaging young trees. The main evidence left of such boundaries in Hooke are on the edges of the two oak coppices for the deer pales. Other produce from such woodland would include hazelnuts and charcoal. Any lime-kilns would have been fired by charcoal (oak charcoal burning at a higher temperature) so the two oak coppices probably came into their own after the deer park ceased to exist. The income from woodland, the largest proportion of the income coming from the underwood, was greater than that from arable land and only a little less than from meadow. The value of wood stayed roughly in line with income, but the supply was limited without raiding hedges.

By this time the underwood from the woods and coppices may not have been sufficient for local requirements. It was not uncommon to supplement the supply from hedgerows. The dating of hedgerows is difficult, although formulae do exist. Certainly some of the hedgerows in the parish would appear to be several hundred years old. Very few hedges in the parish run in straight lines (except where following obvious land features such as streams or tops of hills), possibly suggesting that they were in existence before 1700. There are also many coppice stools and large pollard trees. Maple is common amongst the hedgerows. These hedgerows would have been well maintained until about 1870.

Enclosure

In about 1620 the Marquis of Winchester, Sir Francis Fulford, Sir Thomas Trenchard and Roger Preston agreed to divide up and enclose the wastes of Hooke, Poorton, Wytherston, Toller Porcorum and Kingcombe, though the plan was not carried through. The plan seems to have been implemented later in the century.

Agricultural Fairs

Agricultural fairs continued throughout this period and Stapleford still had permission for a fair. The location is not clear, but it might have been on Toller Down in what is shown as Fair Field.

Chapter 6

Paulets:
The Dukes of Bolton from the end of the Civil War to the Earls of Sandwich and the Dukes of Cleveland
(1660-1827)

National Background and Village Structure

Nationally

In 1660 Charles II became king. He is considered to have been a weak king with poor foreign policy advisers. He worked through parliament. He had no children from his wife, although plenty from his many mistresses! In 1665 there was the Great Plague of London followed in 1666 by the Great Fire of London. The Whig and Tory party systems originate from 1679.

In 1685 James II, Charles II's brother became king. Charles II kept his Roman Catholic sympathies quiet, but James lost his job at the Admiralty because of his sympathies. The Duke of Monmouth, an illegitimate son of Charles II, was the potential replacement for James and landed at Lyme Regis at the start of the Monmouth Rebellion. The Duke of Monmouth hoped to seize the crown from James II. He is reputed to have refreshed his troops in the village of Hooke, on his way to the fatal Battle of Sedgemoor where the rebels were defeated. Judge Jeffries then presided over the "Bloody Assizes" at Dorchester where 230 were executed, several hundred transported and even more died in prison. There was more religious persecution of Protestants and James packed Parliament with his own supporters.

In 1689 William of Orange, married to Mary (the niece of Charles II), landed at Brixham and there was a further Civil War that was won by William. James tried to regain power at the Battle of the Boyne in Ireland but was defeated. William was the champion of Protestantism. He was declared king by parliament and was the first constitutional monarch to reign jointly with his wife. However, there were still problems with Spain and with Scotland.

In 1702 Anne became queen. She had 17 children by her husband Prince George of Denmark, but none survived. Marlborough was winning battles at Blenheim, Ramilles, and Ordernarde for 10 years until The Treaty of Utrecht brought an end to these hostilities with the Dutch. It was a time of well-known names in literature, science and architecture such as Swift, Pope, Addison, Steele, Locke, Newton and Wren.

With no obvious heir to the throne there was another parliamentary decision on the succession with a requirement for a Protestant. George I of Hanover became king, but never learned English. He brought with him a wife and two mistresses. His wife was kept in strict confinement on suspicion of adultery! The affairs of government were left to his ministers, mainly Whig at this time. Walpole was the first Prime Minister.

George II became king in 1727 and his Queen Caroline was a clever adviser and he was devoted to her. Walpole set up cabinet government. George II was the last monarch to lead the army into battle. 1756 was the start of the Seven Years' War against France, leading to great British losses. Pitt the Elder became Prime Minister.

George III became king in 1760, a turbulent reign. Extra taxes were levied on N. America leading to the 1775 War of Independence. There was an element of personal rule towards the end of the previous king, but this came to an end in 1783 with a larger role for Parliament. Pitt the younger became Prime Minister in that year. The Napoleonic Wars were from 1783 – 1804 and had some impact on Hooke. In 1811 the king was unwell, being considered "mad". His son, the Prince Regent ruled. It was the time of the great military leaders: Wellington and Nelson. In 1801 Ireland was unified with England. In 1807 the slave trade was abolished, which had provided a lucrative income to some Dorset families, one of whose successors lived in Hooke. Cultural figures of the time included the authors Byron, Jane Austin, Shelley, Keats and the artist Gainsborough. George IV came to the throne in 1820 and was an extravagant, immoral king.

The modern calendar came into being in 1752, although the number of days in the year and the use of leap years had been in existence since 46 AD.

The Role of Magistrates

The pikes that had been supervised by the magistrates for use against the Armada were brought out again in 1804 for the Volunteers against Napoleon.

Hooke Court

The owners now held the title of Dukes of Bolton. The first two dukes appear to have been absentee landlords with little interest in Hooke. It was much repaired by the 3rd Duke of Bolton who resided there.

The church

There seems to have been relatively little further changes to the church, worship and the involvement of the villagers until about the middle of the 18th century. The order and layout of the church was changed to enable the preaching of the word to take precedence over the sacrament. A multi-deck pulpit would have been introduced (probably only two tiers in a small village church or side by side pulpits at different levels). There could have been box pews in the south aisle for the landowner, and possibly box pews or a mixture in the nave.

The village

In 1662 the hearth tax identifies a "New Park House". The new house could be a residence associated with the new Deer Park (such as Keepers Lodge or Hunters Lodge), or it could have been Park Pond Cottage with its own set of small fields overlooking Park Pond. Park Pond Cottage was destroyed in about 1970 after becoming derelict to enable the opening up of the current large field there. There is a photograph of the cottage before demolition in the County Museum.

1670 sees one of the last mentions of Stapleford, when there is mention of a cottage and a croft at Stapleford. Perhaps Stapleford resembled Salway Ash and Bowood with a scattering of farmsteads, so did one of the farmhouses become the Mason's Arms?

The Land Tax and the County Rate were as follows:
1682 Eggardon Hundred Divisions: Hooke and Witherston
Land Tax:

Tithing	Parish
£92 8s	£92 8s

1740 Eggardon Hundred Divisions: Hooke and Witherston
County Rate:

Tithing	Parish
19s 3d	19s 3d

In both cases the two figures are identical, so presumably these were a further taxation burden on the poor residents of Hooke in addition to the normal tithes.

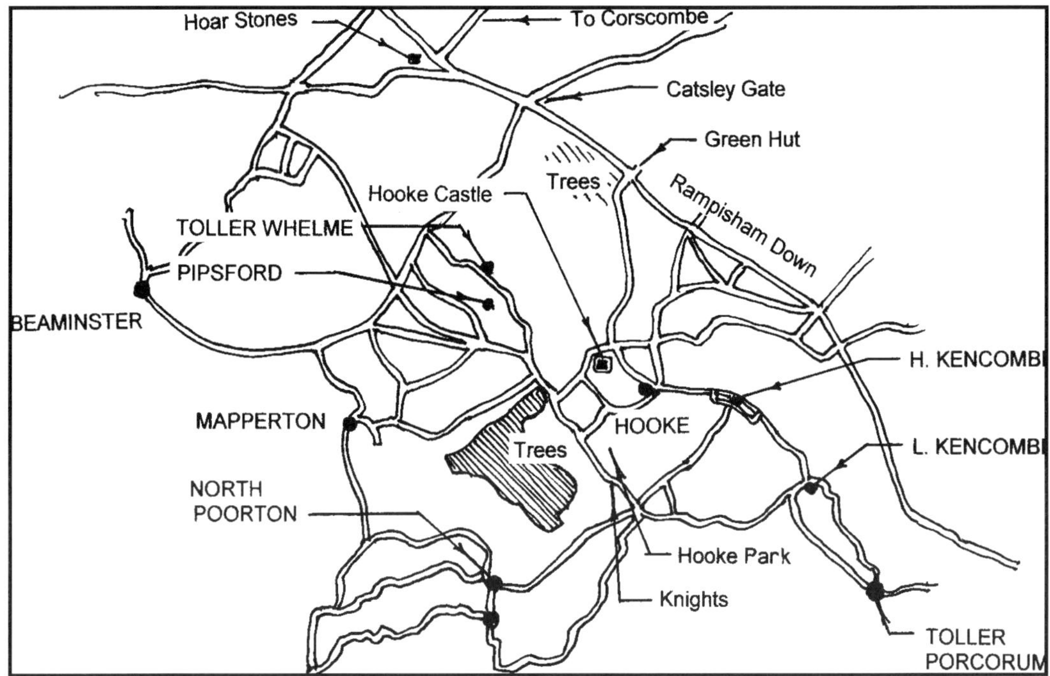

Figure 6.1 **Isaac Taylor's map of the area**

In Isaac Taylor's map (Figure 6.1) note the position of Hooke Park suggesting that the deer park was no longer on Toller Down but between the village and Warren Hill. The circular track around "Hooke Castle" does not seem to agree with any other maps, unless the loop on the south west side was the footpath that existed until the 1950s. The track from Hooke to Green Hut can still be found in part as the bridleway that does a sharp turn to the right to join Linnet Lane today.

It is certain that the two settlements of the village were in full use by the end of this period. The drawing based on an Ordnance Survey map (Figure 6.2) shows the two parts quite clearly. In addition the road from Hooke Court to Hooke Park is already in place, and has also been shown in Isaac Taylor's map. Knights-in-the-Bottom has not yet got the current title, but is just Knights (or Knights Bottom on some sources), supporting the idea that it was where one spent nights (in the Mason's Arms). The roads shown are more akin to current bridleways than current roads, some of which did not exist at that time. The track from Chalk

Corner across to the Rampisham masts is shown on Good's maps (1944) as Parsonage Coppice Drove appearing to go on to Sandhill. Good also shows the main parts of the two roads that ran through the valley from Hooke to Toller Porcorum.

There have been many 18th and 19th century pottery sherds found on sites where houses have been built in the last thirty years. The settlement nearer to the church has a clear triangular area showing on the tithe map (copy on display in St. Giles church and a copy is held in the Beaminster Museum, the original being in the Dorset Record Office). The area appears to have a lane on each side. There were properties (some of barely hovel dimensions) on all sides, although Back Lane leading to Green Lane seems to be the least populated.

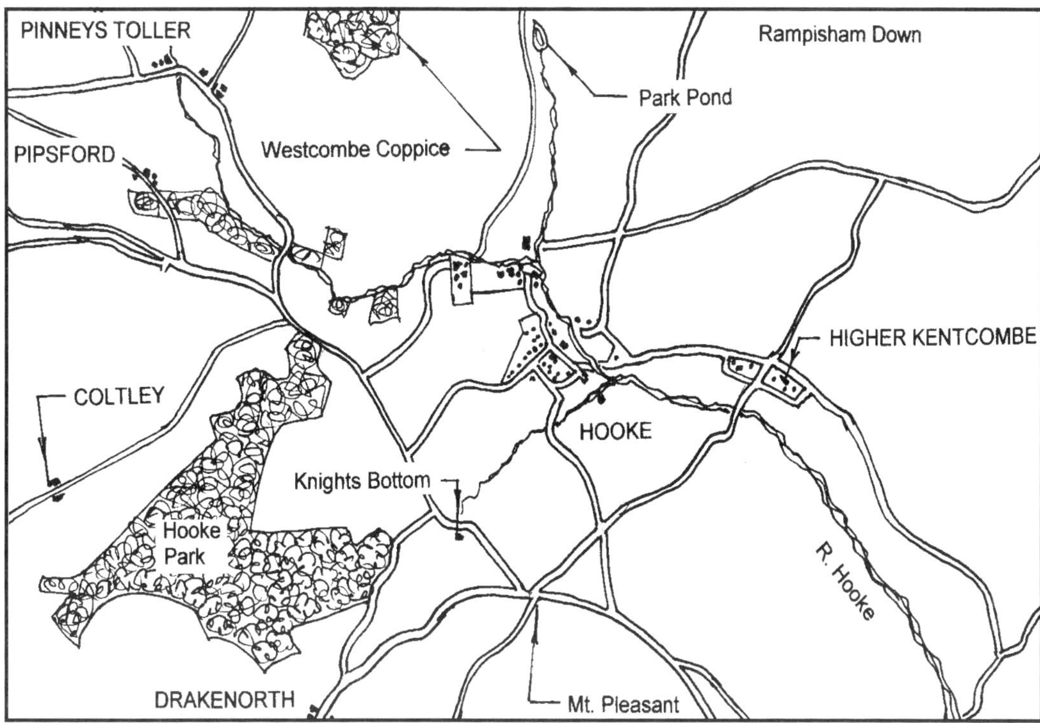

Figure 6.2 **Features shown on the 1811 O. S. map**

There is no road from the church towards Rampisham Hill; the current road was built on the old route of the leat. The other area of settlement is based on Hooke Court; it consisted of the manor house, a mill, a farm and cottages including the blacksmiths. The platform on which the court is built extends to the west and to the east.

The properties in Hooke were mostly small and often had landless occupants such as agricultural labourers who had gardens often not adjacent to their property. An excavation of the site where Forge Cottage now stands produced a few post medieval sherds of pottery amongst a small number of medieval sherds. The site and that next door appear to have been excavated or quarried for some purpose in the past. Perhaps it had become a rubbish dump later.

Much of the field system that existed at this time (shown on the tithe map 13 years later) still exists today. In the church there is an aerial photograph taken in 2000 for comparison with the tithe map and much of the old field system is recognisable. Hooke Park has more recently extended over what was pasture by the road leading to Warren Hill. At the time of the tithe map a large block of land belonged to the estate, the remainder of the land was either a patchwork quilt of ownership or had strips belonging to particular owners.

There were doss houses on the left hand side of the road going down to Knights-in-the-Bottom (one clear cottage outline, Hunters Lodge on the Tithe Map, can still be seen surrounded by a profusion of snowdrops early each year) and a farmhouse, the foundations of which are still in the adjoining field. Local tradition has it that the doss houses were for drovers, there being no accommodation at the Masons Arms. The doss houses were "served by women of the village".

Smugglers

The smugglers route from the coast went towards Corscombe and then on to Bristol and Bath. Isaac Gulliver, the king of the smugglers, lived at North Eggardon Farm. It seems highly likely that the smugglers would have come through Powerstock and some part of Hooke (the Masons Arms is reported as a smugglers' inn). The route would then have carried on to the Jolly Sailor, another smugglers' inn, where the current Rampisham Garage exists. One source (Penrose, 1964) states "Being off the beaten track, it is reported that when smuggling was rife at West Bay, the hands of some of Hook's inhabitants were not above reproach".

Individuals of Interest

Dukes of Bolton, the Duke of Cleveland and the Earl of Sandwich

During this period a sequence of 7 dukes and an earl were the owners of Hooke Court.

The 6th Marquis of Winchester became the Duke of Bolton a year after the restoration of the monarchy by marrying the illegitimate daughter of the Earl of Sunderland "the Scropes family of ancient line" … implying that the Paulets were not! Hackwood Park, the seat of Lord Bolton later, was the hunting lodge of Basing House.

The second Duke of Bolton, when Earl of Wiltshire, played an active part in the revolution of 1688, coming over with William from The Hague.

The 3rd Duke married an actress; he already had three illegitimate sons. He made alterations and improvements to Hooke Court. The title went to his brother as the 4th Duke because the 3rd Duke had no legitimate heirs; the 4th Duke had two sons each of whom became the Duke, but neither produced any heirs. Harry, the 6th Duke, died in 1794 without issue. The title of Marquis of Winchester passed to George Paulet of Amport. Mary, the first daughter of Harry, married John Montagu, the 5th Earl of Sandwich. Catherine, the second daughter of Harry by his second wife married William Vane the 4th Duke of Cleveland. The Paulet estates were shared between these two families.

Minterne family

The Minterne family, already mentioned in previous chapters, regularly attended the manorial court from 1708 to 1838. The family still lived in Hooke until the 20th century. A member of the family who emigrated from England to Australia left a legacy called the Mintern Trust to help poor people in the village. The Trust still exists today.

Popes

William Pope came into the possession of Kingcombe in the late 17th century. He had four sons: Ezekiel (1673-1735) who was a tenant of George Richards who had acquired Toller Whelme (and almost immediately became Sherriff of Dorset in 1710); John (1718 –1793); Thomas (1721-1797); and William (1734-1760). The Popes leased or owned several thousand acres (including land in Hooke) in the 18th and 19th centuries rearing sheep for wool. Mary Pope (1729 - ?) married Henry Legg.

The Popes also owned mills and factories at Hooke and Beaminster. The name appears as members of Manorial Court records of Hooke from 1789 to 1823. In 1796 William Pope married his first cousin Sarah Legg. They purchased Toller Whelme outright from John Richards.

William Pope was pious and built the church at Toller Whelme, in the parish of Corscombe, at his own personal expense – designing it himself and he supervised all the work. The cost of building the church ruined William Pope. Mrs Keddle, the wife of the Rector of Hooke, provided the cushions for the altar. The church was consecrated on June 7th 1871. The benefice was in the gift of the Reverend W. J. Pope a grandnephew of William. In 1872 it was given to the Rector of Hooke, the Reverend Robert Keddle, with a stipend of £40 per annum. The estate went into the hands of trustees but was unable to support itself and fell into the hands of mortgagers. The inhabitants fought for many years to return the parish into Corscombe and they were eventually successful in 1920 when Benjamin Childs bought Toller Whelme. However the transfer had to wait until the incumbent rector of Hooke retired or died and that eventually took place in 1939.

Hines of Beaminster

Thomas Hine of Beaminster, merchant, took over the fulling mill from the Minternes and the Fords in 1797 but relinquished it in 1805. It would seem that his ownership followed that of the Popes.

Interactions affecting people in the village

Defence for Napoleon's expected invasion

Dorset found itself on the front line of national defence at the end of the 18th century. There was a threat of invasion from Napoleon's army. Most elaborate arrangements were made in the event of an invasion. There was an added problem that King George III often stayed at Weymouth, the potential front line. The Dorset Yeomanry was founded in 1794 and volunteer forces were raised to supplement the army and the militia. As has already been identified, the pikes were at the ready under the control of the magistrates. There were arrangements for people, animals and goods to be moved inland in case of an invasion and everyone knew the route to be taken. The map shows the depots for removing "live and dead animals" (Figure 6.3). It seems likely that the number shown alongside Hooke is an identification number. It is not clear where the depot was in Hooke or what would be done with the "dead animals".

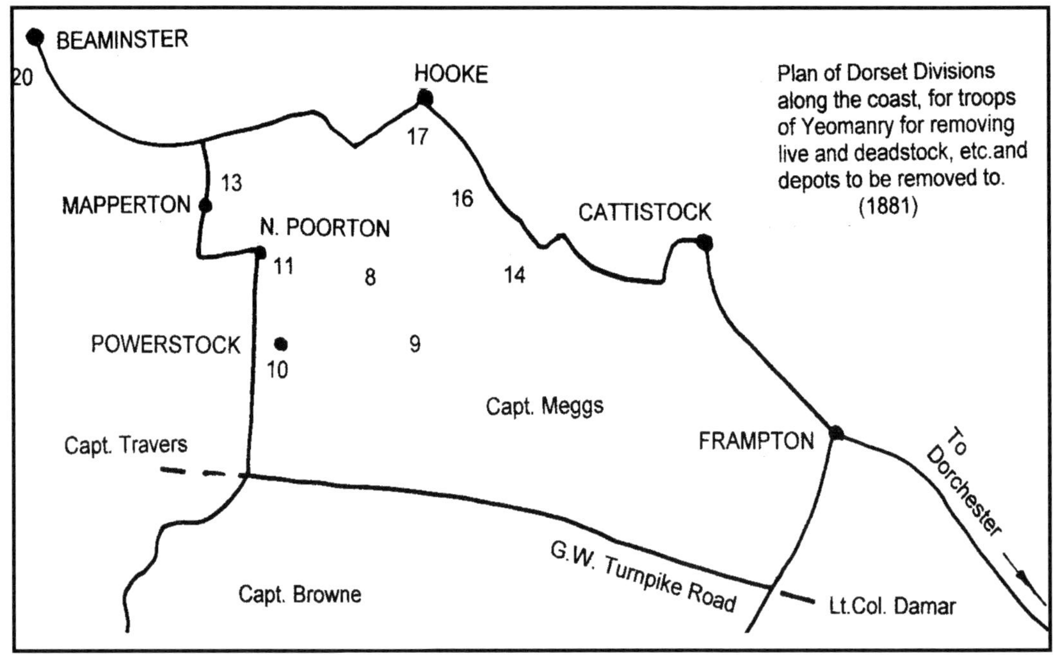

Figure 6.3 **Extract from the map of Dorset Divisions along the coast (1881)**

Manorial Court Records

The Manorial Court records of this period are available in the Dorset County Record office. From 1700 onwards they have some interesting entries. Details of the stewards, tithingmen (changed to hayward in 1732) and attendees at the courts are in Appendix A. Although women had previously been told to provide the hayward (assumed to be male), in 1765 Ann Randall was the first recorded woman hayward.

In 1715 the tucking mill was out of repair and wood was needed for the maintenance. In 1719 John Williams, the miller had become tithingman. Is he the miller for the tucking mill or a gristmill? Did the mill carry out two purposes or are there two mills by this time? As timber is required for the gristmill in 1724 it confirms by this time there were two mills. Further evidence of two mills occurs when timber was allowed for the mills in 1725, again in 1727 (this year specifying for fulling mill and grist mill) and in 1731. By 1743 timber is again required for the mill and in 1744 Samuel Minterne is allowed timber to repair the mills (Samuel Minterne has been previously identified as yeoman, but no mention of the mills becoming his). Timber requested for the tucking mill in 1762, 1763, and for both mills in 1782 (although the steward protested), 1783, and 1784 (still in need of repair). By 1805 there is a further request for timber for the mills.

From the many entries in the early 18th century there is obviously a pound that is out of repair. There is no record of the location of the pound, although it was normal for a village to have one. The entries continue in 1740 with “some bars wanting in the pound”, 1751, 1754 (still out of repair), and in 1762.

In 1709 there was a bridge required at Moulham’s house. Presumably the house was by the river somewhere and the court required it to be built. By 1715 a tree had been allocated to make the bridge by which time widow Moolam (note the inconsistency in spelling) had died.

In 1745 the church bridge is presented as out of repair. This suggests that the leat in front of the church already existed and that the mill behind the current Paulet House was there. Had the tucking mill been relocated here or was this the gristmill? The next year two bridges are presented as out of repair although the second one is unknown. In 1750, 1751, 1753, 1754, 1756, 1757, 1758, 1759, 1760 (protested against by the steward), 1761, 1762, and 1763 there is a request to have timber to build a bridge to go to the mill (no indication of which mill); as no further requests occurs it would seem that patience succeeded. In 1782 there is a request for timber for both bridges (protested against), again in 1783 and 1784 (out of repair). The request for two bridges to mills to be repaired does suggest that there may have been a third mill. By 1802 and 1805 the bridges are again out of repair and the Lady is to find rough timber.

Sometimes houses are out of repair. 1710 Widow Cornick's house is out of repair; Henry Williams' in 1728; John Davidon's in 1731. The latter is given 3 months to repair it on the forfeiture of 10d. Joan Harden's house needs repairing in 1736 and again in 1737 it is to be "amended" by Mithas (Michaelmas) penalty 40d but is still out of repair in 1738, 1739, and 1740. John Harding's cottage was out of repair in 1740, Widow Cornick's house out of repair 1775, 1797 Portland House, now Bedwell's out of repair, 1804 Henry Cornick's house is out of repair, 1805 Mary Randall's house, Henry Cornick's house and the dwelling house in Bolsons Tenement much out of repair.

At other times fires have occurred. In 1757 William Hallett and Betty his wife are presented for suffering their house to fall down and the materials thereof to be burnt and destroyed; (in 1758 and 1759 the house belonging to the estate of Elizabeth Hallett – perhaps suggesting that they have both died? – "is down and the fences greatly out of repair"). In 1805 the dwelling house on William Leg's Tenement was lately burnt down. Houses fell down or were re-built without permission. In 1806 the mill and the mill house held by William Silk were burnt down since the last court. One suggestion is that the miller was found 40 years later and transported, but there does not seem to be any formal evidence.

The names of other villages and towns associated with people's names on the Manorial Court records are also of interest:

Abraham Everett Yeoman of Tollard (is this Tollard Royal etc. or Toller?);
William Crane Yeoman of Mapperton;
Deptford appears too, along with St. Clement Danes (an ironmonger!):
William Bartlett of Roddon in Dorset;
Jacob Pitfields of Simesbury;
Thomas Pope of Corscombe;
Thomas Hine of Beaminster;
Thomas Fry of Litton Cheney;
Charles Powlett (clerk) of Warren Street in Middlesex (represented by Theophilus Bartlett, attorney);
John Thompson, gentleman of Bath (through attorney John Symes of Bridport);
Robert White, surgeon, of Dorchester;
Sarah Tucker of Lyme Regis;
John Tucker, gentleman, of Chard;
Richard Bridge of Langdon, Beaminster;
Benjamin Follett of The Temple, London;
Charles Ganmes of Axminster.

An entry in 1725 shows William Legg (Yeoman of Hooke) not only becomes a copyholder of a cottage and garden but also 40 acres(!) out of the waste.

In 1802, the same year that William Pope purchased the Toller Whelme estate, Theophilus Bartlett of Hooke bought the 400 acre Pipsford Farm which he sold on to Peter Cox, a Beaminster solicitor; in turn he sold it to Admiral Robert Aitcheson who in his turn sold it to the Popes in 1855.

Various fines were imposed on named people in Hooke, some of whom attended the court when the fines were imposed. (The symbols "s" means old shillings, "d" old pence.)

1715 Thomas Williams for not stowing up of his ditch – ordered to "browse" ditch before Lady Day penalty 9d.
1719 John Williams, miller, for letting his pigs run about the common amortize 1d
1720 Benjamin Williams for over grazing the common amortize 1d. John Williams for letting his horses abide on the common by night amortize 5d.
1733 there is a comment that horses are still on the common, 6d each night.
1751 amorze 3d those not appearing this day at court.
1755 Samuel Brown (who had attended the manorial court the previous year) has depasturised his horses on the commons of the manor having no right of common and he is amortized 20s (*a very large sum).*
1768 Mr Chilcott for not making up his fence against widow Crane's orchard called Shorts – amorze him 13s 4d.
1769 The hedge between Shorts orchard and Mr Chilcott's garden be down and to be repaired by Mr Chilcott before Christmas under ye penalty of 20s (*a very large sum).*
1771, 1772, 1773 William Durnford for an encroachment (*a dwelling?)* on the Lord's waste – in 1773 if not taken down by 1st Sept. next - we amorze him 40s.
1771 Samuel Jakes for erecting a cottage on the Duke's farm, Hooke Farm.
1775 Widow Orchard, William Durnford and William Legg for not taking away an encumbrance on the waste land…. Each 40s (*a very large sum).*

In 1791 the following were present at the Manorial Court for encroachments: Thomas Rupshells, garden in the common, John Short (garden), William Durnford (garden), Thomas Hutchins, Mary Day, Edward Rupshell, William Cole, Mary Rebdell, Widow Bridge. In 1794 Thomas Rupsells again has garden in the common. In 1809 Robert Hallett and William Bartlett were presented for "diging" sand on the waste of the Manor and being tenant.

In 1735 Samuel Minterne, Mrs Mary Minterne, Sarah Everett are present for not keeping up their bounds against Ramsam (now called Rampisham) Down and if they do not amend in a month's time will amorze them 10s.

From 1809 onwards some new dwellings get mentioned:

1809: north side of lane leading to Knights-in-the- Bottom (first record of this name);
1810: cottage 20' x16' in Green Lane;
1810: cottage on the waste in Green Lane;
1810: *(a second)* cottage 20' x 16' on the waste in Green Lane.

These new dwellings in Green Lane were probably either on the West side of Green Lane or on the triangle by Back Lane, probably the former judging by the size from the tithe map because each had a garden and appurtenances.

All land and property was copyhold until about 1925. There were three holders named, when one copyholder died a new name could be added by the payment of a fine. The landlords made most of their money by the system of fines. The list of fines were produced about every 20 years based on surveys of the land carried out. It was a sort of actuarial decision predicting required income for the next 20 years.

Occupations are not often recorded. There are several entries of yeoman. In 1745 there was a John Legg, mason. By the early 19th century there are many labourers mentioned.

Agriculture

Hayward

An important person in the records of the manorial court was the tithingman or hayward. No other official gets mentioned. The hayward therefore probably covered three roles in a small village: hayward, reeve, constable or beadle. The beadle was the policeman of the village, taking pledges, levying fines for behavioural misdemeanours. In some references he is referred to as the hedgewarden. Hedges were not permanent, but were temporary and reset every two years protecting from cattle the part of the common land that was under tillage. When the field was restored to fallow the hedge was removed. The hayward had an important role being in charge of all the operations concerned with sowing and harvesting of crops. The hayward needed to be a sharp man who would look after and go round the woods, corn and meadows. He was in charge of the ploughers and harrowers and would either do or be in charge of the sowing. At hay time he would supervise the mowers and the making and carrying of hay. At harvest time he would assemble the reapers and labourers and check that all was safely gathered in and that none was stolen or spoilt. He organised the day at hay time and at harvest time. He would go from door to door reminding the villagers that they were required the next day. He would divide them into groups and place them in different parts of the field. He would move from place to place seeing that all was well. He would blow a horn at lunchtime to indicate a break for food and drink. At the end of the day he would sound the horn for cessation from work when all would go to the manor house for a good evening meal, the hayward sitting with other manorial officers. Any misdemeanours would be brought before the bailiff to be heard at the manorial court if necessary. He usually had his rent excused or lowered or was given an allotment in the common land.

Livestock

In 1736 Samuel Minterne had permission to use 24 acres in the common fields and common pasture for 150 sheep. Sheep would have been important for most of this period. The sheep would have been up on the chalk land (usually common land) during the day with a common shepherd and brought down into the valleys at night into folds – arable land areas surrounded by hazel hurdles. The whole process was controlled by the manor. The idea was that the sheep would fertilise the area inside the fold. The sheep would move about 10 miles each day and had a limited life. The wool and meat were by-products from the main purpose. Dorset Horn and Dorset Poll sheep were ideal because they were docile and could breed at any time of the year. With the advent of fertilisers in the 19th century the Dorset Poll and Dorset Horn sheep had become more important for wool.

Cattle would be fattened and both sheep and cattle would be taken by drovers along the many drovers' ways to market (these ways can still be identified on the Ordnance Survey maps). There would be pubs along the way with a cluster of small fields where the drovers could "park" their animals and get food and rest. Such inns included the Masons Arms at Knights-in-the-Bottom at Hooke, and the Jolly Sailor at the top of Rampisham Hill (where the current garage is sited) already mentioned in connection with smugglers.

John Ogilvy's 1698 **Brittania** (one of the earliest road atlases) confirms the position where the Deer Park abuts the current main road (Figure 6.4), but by this time it was a remnant, the rest having been destroyed by the widespread abuse identified in the Standing Committee minute book.

The old deer park had probably become unusable after the Commonwealth period. The deer park seems to have moved to a location between Hooke Court and the track over Warren Hill. There were two cottages generally shown as Keepers Lodge and Hunters Lodge that may have been at the extreme ends. Keeper's Lodge was by the T-junction by Hooke Park and Hunters Lodge about half way down the hill to Knights-in-the-Bottom. Both locations now have a profusion of snowdrops and the foundations of the cottage can still be seen for Hunters Lodge. The extent of the site is not clear on any map, although it appears to straddle Green Lane, the main track into Hooke at the time. No obvious deer pales can be seen, but there is a double hedge on a bank for the top stretch of Green Lane. It is possible that the causeway across the field at Warren Hill that was excavated as a possible Roman road could have been one of the deer pales.

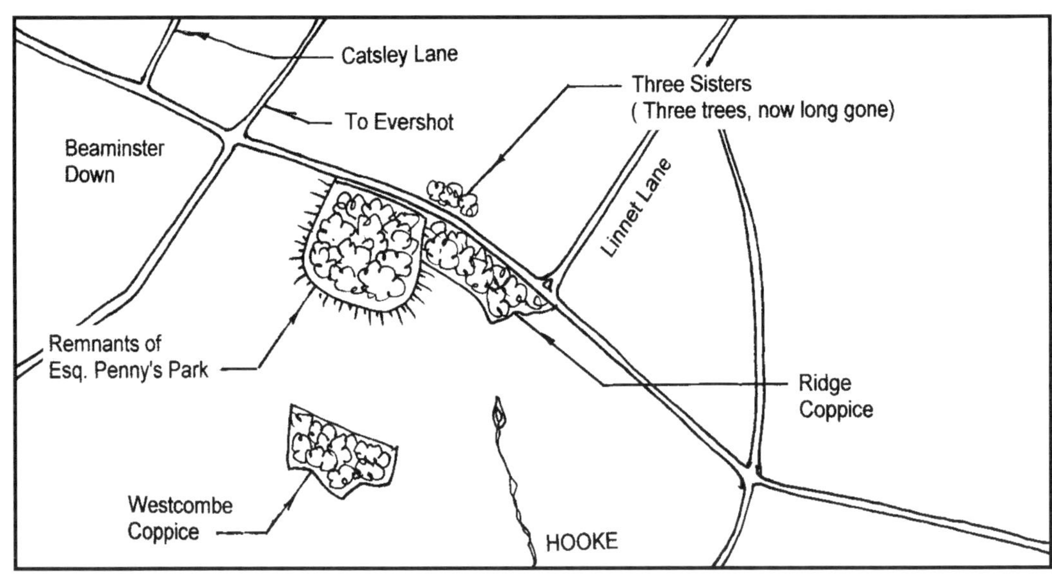

Figure 6.4 **Features shown on Ogilvy's map (1698)**

Taylor's 1795 map shows Hooke Park in the intermediate position. By the 1811 O. S. map it is on the current site, although the woodland was not so extensive. There is evidence of deer pales in the woods of Hooke Park; the easiest to see is alongside the Jubilee Trial footpath near the road leading from Hooke to North Poorton. The alternative explanation for this ditch and bank could be a parish boundary, but it does not appear to coincide with known parish boundaries. The park was still referred to as "the deer park" during the time that the Salts who lived at Hooke in the early 20th century.

The woodlands around Hooke have been there for at least 700 years and in some cases 1000 years even though some have been felled and replanted several times.

Lime kilns

There was a fairly large lime kiln at Hooke (Map reference ST 52780074). The kiln is no longer in existence. The site was alongside a large chalk pit filled in after the Second World War to extend the field for grazing (although the field has occasionally been used for crops). Lime kilns in Dorset for agricultural purposes date back to the 16th century, although the origins of the one at Hooke are not clear. The limekiln would almost certainly have been in use by the late 18th century at the latest and probably went on being used until the early 20th century. Most lime burners were farmers. The lime would have been used in building and for lime wash waterproofing of buildings. Lime was considered to be manure by the earlier writers and improvers for agriculture. It was used alongside chalk and marl for improving the soil.

It seems probable that Westcombe Coppice was a source of oak for charcoal that would enable a temperature of 900^{0}C necessary to decompose the chalk. The chalk would yield about half its weight in quicklime that reacts violently with water to produce hydrated lime (about 100 times as soluble as limestone). The lime was taken from the kiln and allowed to slake in a corner of a field. It was progressively ploughed or harrowed in (usually in Spring or Autumn) to neutralise soil acidity. Donkeys were used for the transportation from the limekiln using the route of the bridleway that comes out by Juniper Cottage.

Lime was also used for mortar where slaked lime was added to sand. For Dorset cottages lime wash was used for laying hard floors being an improvement on beaten earth. Whitewash was also made from lime and whiting. Details of Dorset limekiln types can be found in the paper by Stanier.

Agricultural fairs

In 1662 George Penne (the same mentioned on the map earlier in the chapter as Penny) was granted a charter to hold a fair on Toller Down from the last day of August for five days. In 1689 the Pennes had another charter to hold a fair between 18th and 25th May. The fairs created a source of income for the estate that had suffered badly under sequestration. It would appear that the Pennes had in someway become tenants of the estate. Owens New Book of Fairs in 1845 gives the following information: the May fair was for the sale of bullocks, sheep and horses (and was popular with Irish horse dealers); the July fair for the sale of sheep and lambs; the September fair for the sale of bullocks, sheep and horses (so by this time the dates had changed from August). Agricultural fairs drew buyers and sellers from a wide area, a 15-mile radius covered most of the buyers and sellers, but some came from as far away as Pensford, near Bath, Shaftesbury and Weymouth. Fairs were also an excuse for people to have a good time so provided general recreation.

The fair was held in Fair Field and in the middle of the field was a single storey stone pavilion (the date of construction is unknown). The pavilion was where much business was carried out and many meals served. Around the pavilion were pens for livestock. The pavilion was destroyed by fire in 1903.

Chapter 7

Dukes of Cleveland and Earls of Sandwich
(1827-1917)

National Background and Village Structure

Nationally

In 1830 William IV, an unassuming, popular king who led an exemplary private life, succeeded George IV. In 1833 slavery was abolished in the British Colonies. The Poor Law was reformed for the first time since 1601 leading to the setting up of workhouses. In 1835 Local Government was reformed.

William's niece, Victoria, became queen in 1837. She was married to Prince Albert who was described as tactless, serious, conscientious and very German! Some writers considered him to have been the virtual ruler through influence. From 1842 women and children were not allowed to work in the mines. In 1851 the Crystal Palace Exhibition took place, largely influenced by Albert, and the profits were used to set up the Victoria and Albert Museum, the Science Museum, the Imperial College of Science and Technology, the Royal College of Music and the Royal Albert Hall – quite an achievement! Further legislation included the Public Health Act, 1875 and the Trades Union Acts 1871, 1876, each of which would have had some effect on Hooke. New Zealand, Canada, Australia became part of the Empire with the sales of lamb and wool affecting British agriculture. The Crimean War was from 1853 to 1856 and the Boer Wars took place in 1881 and 1899 – 1902.

The Boer War had a surprising effect on Hooke. 51 wounded officers from the British and Commonwealth convalesced at Hooke Court, being looked after by the Earl with the assistance of a masseur.

Queen Victoria died in 1901 and Edward VII became king, although neither his father nor his mother had considered him really suitable. He raced yachts and horses (one of which won the Derby). He was an active expert in foreign affairs. The *Entente Cordiale* was agreed with France in 1904. Old Age Pensions were introduced in 1908 and the Labour Exchange instituted in 1909.

King George V, who had trained as a naval officer, became king in 1910, the second son of Edward VII. The king visited the front during the First Great War, 1914 – 1918, in which several people from Hooke served. The king suffered severe internal injuries in 1915 when his horse rolled on him and never fully recovered.

Hooke Village

In 1801 the manorial courts elected constables but by 1857 there was a unified county constabulary service, Hooke having its own police station in what is now Ivy Cottage. The old police lamp still stands on the wall outside the cottage.

In 1840 parishes maintained the roads and by 1901 there were gravelled tracks linking villages.

The administration of the countryside was by two JPs who came together four times each year at Quarter Sessions for administrative and judicial functions. The JPs replaced the tithing system by this time. By 1888 elected County Councils were in control. Parish Councils came into existence in 1894, Hooke electing to have a Parish Meeting, as it still does.

By 1836 Dorset was transferred back to the Diocese of Salisbury. In 1885 Kelly described the church of St. Giles as "a very ancient Gothic structure". Medieval churches lacked care and had become dilapidated in spite of occasional repairs. It seems that St. Giles was no exception and the church was repaired in 1844.

For most of the 19th century Hooke Court was a farmhouse. The Royal Commission on Historic Monuments describe two tenements 260 yards south east of the church with two-storey walls of rubble and roofs slate; these were approximately where the current houses Kingfishers and Springfield now stand. It seems possible that one of these original tenements was the site of the third mill. According to the Hunt and Co Directory the population was 268 in 1841. The population in 1871 was 202.

On the tithe map there were cottages on the west side of Green Lane all the way up to The Buildings. There were also cottages on Back Lane from Green Lane to the village green. There was a farm and an inn, The Masons Arms, at Knights-in-the-Bottom. In 1841 John Legg was the landlord of The Masons' Arms and he was also the Parish Clerk. The footings of the Masons Arms at Knights-in-the-Bottom can be seen near the wooden hut. There were 7.5 acres of small fields, but no accommodation. There were cottages on the north side of the lane leading down to Knights-in-the-Bottom. Most of the cottages were made from rubble or were cob. It seems likely that some were even less substantial, perhaps still using wattle and daub! There were one and two room hovels, judging by their location on the tithe map of 1840.

School

The National Society for the Promoting Education of the Poor in the Principles of the Established Church was established in 1811. The purpose of any school under its auspices was to enable the reading of the scriptures and understanding the doctrines of the church. By 1870 the Forster Education Act required School Boards to be set up to ensure that schooling became universal through England. The school at Hooke was designed in 1856, so it pre-dated the Forster Act. William Mabey described the school as "Hook Cottage school". It is not clear how the school was funded. Normally the landowner provided some of the finance and the parents contributed according to their means, for example farmers 6d each week, labourers 2d for each week, reducing to 1d each week after the first year. Plans held in the Dorset Record Office show a school with separate entrances for girls and boys and two classrooms with the schoolmistress's house attached. The toilets were by the river and flowed out into it (and were still there just before the Second World War). There were no septic tanks and individual sewage systems at that time. Today there is still no mains drainage in Hooke.

On November 27th 1903 the Earl of Sandwich invited all the children and some of the parents for tea in the schoolroom, Mrs Papillon of Cattistock presiding. After tea the children played games.

There was some sort of night school according to William Mabey " ...I used to attend night school, and had some fine old times fighting with each other"!

Rebuilding of the village

The Earl built a new rectory in 1865. The rectory was built of local dressed stone with stone mullioned windows and a high-pitched slate roof. It had three reception rooms, a kitchen, scullery, and six bedrooms (all but one having grates). There was an outside water closet for the servants. The building was one of the first in Hooke to have water closets, although the outlet pipes to the river got blocked on occasions. There were also stables and a coach house, later converted to a cottage and garage. The stables had three stalls, a harness room and a fodder loft. The rector in 1885 was the Reverend Robert Antram Keddle, B. A. of Jesus College Cambridge.

The Earl largely rebuilt the village from about 1870 onwards. Two bridges were built with double skin brick arches, one of which, Carpenter's Bridge, was strengthened in 2003, the other having been made flat and renovated at an earlier unknown date. The date of Carpenter's bridge is shown with the Sandwich crest on each arch just above the river, dated 1878. Estate cottages were late being built in the centre of the village around the turn of the 20th century.

Shops and post office

Postal services started in 1840 with local pillar-boxes and adhesive stamps following soon after. In 1841 there was a boot and shoemaker (Thomas Cram), a miller and baker (John Crofts). The old post office and shop was built at the turn of the century. By the late 19th century a shop would have had more and varied mass-produced products rather than solely local produce, with the price being reduced.

Mills

In about 1840 Charles Coombs, a millwright, flax and tow spinner from Beaminster, had a twine and thread factory at Hooke. The factory was driven by waterpower, the river being diverted south of the church just inside what is now the south wall of the churchyard. The leat was about 3 metres above the current river bed, suggesting quite a large water wheel.

There were three mills at this time: the original one near Hooke Court, the twine, hemp and thread mill behind the current Paulet House and another flour mill 100 metres downstream, already mentioned in the previous chapter. In 1876 the churchyard was extended on the south side by a gift from the Earl of Sandwich. The site of the "river-bed" between the churchyard and the public road was given to the Parish of Hooke. The addition was approximately 5 metres. A new wall was installed. The "river-bed" was the leat to the mill that had previously existed north of the current site of Paulet House. There is a Faculty referring to this transaction in the Dorset Record Office.

Water supplies

Water was supplied by using hydraulic rams and reservoirs. There is no firm data about when these were installed but it seems likely that they would have accompanied the renovation of Hooke Court for use as a shooting box and been supplied elsewhere in the village at the same time. The water originated from the many springs in Hooke (some authors suggest that these are really Artesian wells). Hydraulic Rams were invented in 1772 by John Whitehurst to pump water to the top floors of his brewery in Oulton, Cheshire. In 1798 Pierre Montgolfier (of the hot air balloon fame) invented an automatic spill valve that made continuous unattended operation possible. Rams have been known to operate for over 100 years without attention. The water is supplied from the spring to a chamber that is at a lower level. The chamber fills with water, escaping through a spring valve and eventually closing it. The water passes through a one-way valve into a second chamber where air is compressed. The air pressure forces water up to a higher level. A back-surge allows the spring valve to re-open and the process is repeated. At least one hydraulic ram was still working in 2003, supplying water to Juniper House.

Changes from 1840 to 1902

There were many chalk pits on the north side of the river, including a large one, now in-filled, in Fire-Brimpton field where there was also a large kiln. Others are shown on the 1890 Ordnance Survey map. Most of these had ceased being used early in the 20th century.

Comparing the 1840 tithe map to the Ordinance Survey map of 1902 shows other considerable changes to Hooke. By 1902 the watercress beds had started to appear although not as extensively as in later years. By 1902 there was a school, a rectory, Bridge Farm, Manor Farm (with its very elaborately and beautifully built barns with well worked lintels of about 1868), Hooke Bridge, Carpenter's Bridge and far fewer houses, particularly around the triangle of Back Lane, Green Lane and what is now Kingcombe Road. The thatched cottages shown on the photograph on display in the church had been replaced by the current two rows of cottages. As will be seen in the table later in the chapter the population had dropped from about 200 to about 150.

At the Hooke Court end of the village many of the cottages had disappeared leaving mainly Hooke Court, the mill, what is now Juniper House and two or three other cottages. Adjacent to Juniper House is an older house now turned into apartments. In the older house, when it was renovated, there was evidence of mullioned windows. Some of the outbuildings that have been converted to holiday cottages also have larges stones and lintels suggesting that an older building had been re-used when they were built.

Excavations at the site of Chelwood prior to its construction unearthed large quantities of 18th and 19th century coarse ware and smaller quantities of fine ware of the same dates. The excavations were on the site of a house shown on the Tithe map of 1840 that had been demolished by 1902.

St. Giles Church and Churchyard

The church silver includes: a Paten 9 inches in diameter given by the Reverend Burgess Lambert in 1827 and a Flagon 8 inches high of the style of a domestic tankard prevalent in seventeenth century. The latter bears, apparently, three makers' names but these are not decipherable.

The church had a gallery that was accessed by outside stairs. The stairs can be seen on the photograph of the church before the modifications of the late 19th century. Looking carefully at the plaster wall above the font the outline of the location of the door can be seen that was at the top of the stairs. There does not appear to have been a west door at this time (see photograph of 1870 church), although the arch and a filled in space can be seen on the photograph.

The church was repaired in 1840 when the chancel was re-built. It would appear that there was some instability of the east wall and two buttresses were put on the northeast and southeast corners of the wall. More recent architects doubt the value of the buttresses.

Further work was carried out in 1874 when the gallery and bell tower were removed, the roof was replaced, the tower built and the west door re-opened; the architect was Mr G. R. Crickmay of Weymouth. In 1874 a vestry was added into which was built one of the 15th century windows. Blanche, the Countess of Sandwich, who died in 1894, paid for the work. It would be at this time that the church was re-ordered with a new layout yet again to meet the expectations for a Church in the late 19th century. It does not quite meet the requirement of having three steps to the altar, but two are obviously more in keeping with the proportions. The new pulpit was placed to the side and the altar becomes a focus because the sacrament becomes more important. The current pews would have been added at this time.

A footbridge, across the leat to the second mill, reached the small churchyard that had served the church for over 400 years. The original leat can be seen on the photograph that is in the church taken by Richard Hine of Beaminster in 1870 before the church was modified.

The churchyard was considerably extended in the late 19th century. The land that had been a cottage and garden on the tithe map was incorporated into the churchyard at the west end. There is no Faculty at the Dorset Record Office for the transference of the cottage. The new wall would have been built at this time. By 1940 the path into the church was gravel to both the tower entrance and to the west door. There was a simple iron arch over the gate holding an oil lamp. The lamp was smashed during a gale either in late 1941 or early 1942.

Figure 7.1 **Statue of St. Giles by Ben Grassby**

St. Giles and the Deer (details of the story of St. Giles is in Appendix G)

Phyl Hide who used to live in the village quoted the following in an article in Team News "Soon after we arrived in Hooke, a friend – Tony Grassby – called in the church on his way to visit us, and noticed some of his grandfather's work: the little statue of St. Giles and the deer" (Figure 7.1).

A Dorset stonemason Benjamin Grassby carved the statue. In 1878 there was an exhibition in Dorset known as The Dorset Industrial Exhibition that was presided over by the Earl of Shaftesbury. Ben Grassby entered the statue and was awarded first prize in the Class 6 Sculpture and Carving, together with a silver medal that is now the prized possession of Tony Grassby, great grandson of Benjamin; no other prizes were awarded in this class. There are many examples of his carvings, sculptures and memorials in Dorset churches: the corbels in North Poorton church, and work at Beaminster and Toller Whelme churches. St. Giles was a popular medieval saint. He was the patron saint of wayfarers, cripples, and blacksmiths and one of 14 saints in the Book of Common Prayer. St. Francis seems to have replaced St. Giles in more recent times.

Hooke and Thomas Hardy

Thomas Hardy worked for John Hicks, a Dorchester architect who was responsible for a number of designs. Crickmays took over Hicks' practice in 1869, by which time Hardy had moved to London. In 1875 Crickmays did the design and built the new tower at Hooke; the church was restored and almost entirely re-built at the sole expense of the Countess.

In Thomas Hardy's "Far from the Madding Crowd" Hooke is identified with Norcombe. Hardy spent time at Rampisham church and was involved in some of the restoration work that took place there. Norcombe is identified as 'near lonely Toller Down'. The features of Norcombe are said by many authors to be drawn from the imagination but Kay-Robinson (Figure 7.2) says that almost every one of the features is found in the area round Hooke and all that Hardy has done is to edit them into the arrangement that he required – not unusual for his novels.

The road from Hooke to Kingcombe runs in a deep cutting fitting Hardy's road from Norcombe to Dorchester. The route was never a turnpike, the gates were at the cross roads on Toller Down, moved by Hardy to this other road. Norcombe Hill could be any of the hills in the area that are featureless convex slopes of chalk and soil. The beech plantation, that was decaying and dying, may well have vanished, but there are at least three woodlands that answer the topographical requirements: Ridge Coppice, Westcombe Coppice and the plantation near Higher Kingcombe. Perhaps Westcombe has become Norcombe (again a normal Hardy type ruse)? The mill at the foot of the hill would fit Townell Mill, and there were remains of a chalk pit between Westcombe Coppice and the mill, although this is not surmounted by a hedge. There are plenty of other chalk pits, one or two of which do have a hedge. One late resident of Hooke reckons that Gabriel Oaks Cottage was Park Pond Cottage.

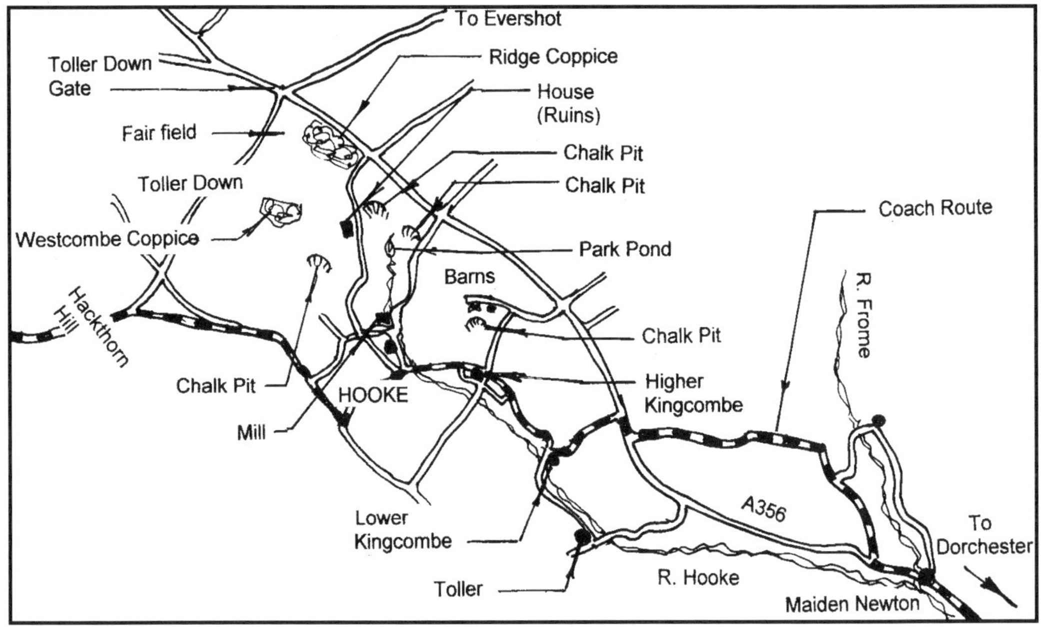

Figure 7.2 **Features shown by Kay-Robinson** (1984)

Individuals of Interest

Earl of Sandwich

The Bolton estates were shared by the Dukes of Cleveland and the Earls of Sandwich, although Hooke was very much the Sandwich's domain. It would appear that it was treated as of little significance until about 1880. For some reason the Earl of Sandwich decided that it would make a good shooting area. The farmer was removed from Hooke Court and was probably the first inhabitant of what is now Manor Farm, earlier called Hooke Farm. Hooke Court was converted into a "shooting box" and parties were held for shooting each year. There would have been some seasonal employment for beaters, etc. It would appear that the Sandwiches spent other times of the year at "Dear Hooke" from the photograph album of their visits held in a private collection. The Earl had a favourite swan that would feed out of his hand.

Rectors

One source states that in 1857 the "Reverend Haviland, Rector of Hooke", went to India as a missionary. He and his six children were murdered in the Indian Mutiny. The source seems to conflict with the list of rectors of Hooke (see Appendix C). The "Reverend Haviland", according to *The History of William Mabey,* was the vicar of Toller Porcorum.

The rector received £49 13s 4d from the tithes on the 1840 Tithe map details. However, prior to the building of the new rectory it is not clear where the rector lived. There are no clues on the tithe map apportionments or from any other records that have come to light to date. The Reverend William Floyer Cornish was paid £44 and £3 glebe rent charge by agreement. However a note adds that an "erroneous supposition that the said rent-charge included a certain prescriptive payment named in the said agreement and that the said agreement as it at present stands would be unjust and if such error as aforesaid had been made known to the said Tithe Commissioners they would have declined to confirm the said agreement..." "I .... James Irwood ...awards ... the sum of forty nine pounds thirteen shillings and four pence ... "

Parish Officers

The parish officers appeared to have the ownership of five plots of land and cottages that were used by Isaac Everett, Ann Hutchins, John Cornick and Daniel Forsey. Daniel Forsey was tithingman from 1837-9 and had previously been tithingman in 1825 and 1826, so this may represent his payment. Clearly there had been a brickyard at some time in Hooke because two plots are entitled *Brick Yard* and *Little Brick Yard.* Some land is still called *Common* and *Higher Common*, although in the ownership and use of Samuel Minterne. There are many interesting names of plots of land perhaps indicating previous use or ownership including: *Salt Moor, Horse Moor, Gallans Hay, Pigs Aldermoor, Pigs, Haycraft Brow, Cockroad, Plough Ground, Warren Hill, Turf Pits* (several), *Starve Acre, Course Ground, Hopyard* (a garden) and *Washing Pond.*

Boer War Officers at Hooke

There are photographs of Hooke Court in use for officers' rehabilitation in the Boer War. "During the South African (War) from Feb 2 (19)00 to Aug 2 (19)02 the Earl of Sandwich received sick and wounded officers at Hinchinbroke Hooke Court. With the assistance of a masseur G Hozier he attended to them entirely himself and as far as possible from the nature of their wounds, they all went away convalescent. The surgical treatment took place at the Misses Keyser Hospital for Officers, 17 Grosvenor Square, London"

There was a VC and other distinguished army decorations amongst those who came. For 47 of the officers the records include a photograph, a signature and brief details of their service in South Africa. Replicas of the document are held in the Beaminster Museum and the National Army Museum. 51 officers came to Hooke Court during that time. Those whose nationality is identified include 24 English, 2 Scottish, 3 Irish, 1 Welsh, 7 South African, 5 Australian, and 3 Canadian. Amongst them was Major C. H. Mullins V. C. of the Imperial Light Horse of Johannesburg, (South African) (Major Mullins was returned to the battlefield in S Africa on two occasions before being so injured that he was sent to England, see Appendix F), Captain Robert Gordon D. S. O. of Stracthcoma's Horse (Australian), Lieut. E. M. D. Fox (Mentioned in Despatches) Yorkshire Light Infantry, and Lieut. Horace Pym (Mentioned in Despatches) of Stracthcoma's Horse (Australian).

The officers stayed varying amounts of time from two days to a series of stays over a period of nine months. Many suffered not only injuries but also enteric fever and dysentery. A Lieut. J. M. Colchester Warmyp of the 7th Dragoon Guards seems to have spent nearly two years trekking around South Africa, eventually being injured by a fall from his horse. All came back by sea and in many cases the name of the ship is also recorded.

Interactions affecting people in the village

Young girls would become members of a family in order to carry out the household chores. It was one of the few ways that girls could earn a living. Sometimes they would sleep in a garrett, sometimes in their mistress's' room and even in their master's room. They could be as young as 12. They would often be recruited by friends and were paid about £2 each year. They would make fires (an early morning job before the rest of the house awoke), clean the grates, fetch the water, empty slops, do much of the family laundry (another early morning chore as early as 2 a.m.), shop for provisions, help with cooking, clear and clean up after meals. When the family became richer they might employ a cook. A maid-of-all-work could be promoted to cook on becoming 21 and earn £4.

The hemp and twine factory

William Mabey, born in 1848 in Beaminster, spent some of his youth in Pound House, Lower Kingcombe and went to school in Toller. Later when the family moved to Higher Kingcombe William and his brother attended the church and school at Hooke. He writes in an account of his life and times that there was a factory in Hooke where hemp and twine were made, and the looms driven by water. As was indicated earlier, the factory belonged to Mr Coombs of Beaminster. When William Mabey left school he went to work in the factory. He carried the bobbins to the looms, taking back the full pones from the women. All the bobbins were turned in the works, and sometimes he would work at the lathe helping the turner. There were about 60 women and girls, and only four men: the engineer (who was also the manager) and three boys. He did not work there very long because his father wanted him to help in the shop at Kingcombe.

The factory girls wore crinolines and hats called "flippy flops". One girl who went to church in an extra large crinoline had a problem (Figure 7.3). She could not get into the pew and had to leave church.

Figure 7.3 **Girl in crinoline in church**

As the factory was associated with the hemp and flax mills in Beaminster belonging to Mr Coombs it seems likely that there was also some need to rett the flax and hemp that was probably grown locally. The retting pit was probably by the river using the outflow from the mill leat. The flax and hemp were soaked in water in order to rot the soft tissues and leave the fibre.

In 1860 the manager (foreman) of the factory, who had been there for many years, was asked to leave. He went round the factory asking whether he had done anyone any harm and they all replied in the negative. He then told them that he would die at the factory. Just before his time for leaving he cut this throat, having previously set fire to the building. That was the end of Hooke factory. The factory was behind and parallel to the present Paulet House.

Changes in employment and the workhouse

The rapid industrialisation in the country produced a massive increase in the able-bodied poor, who were mainly farm labourers losing their livelihood to machines. The low wages in the spinning, weaving and rope-making industries produced similar effects. In 1834 The New Poor Law was intended to replace the previous law that had become costly, cruel and unworkable. It is interesting to note that this was a Georgian law and not Victorian as always assumed. The workhouses assumed that people were idle from choice. The aims of workhouses were:

- to economise by reducing the money given in "out relief", placing paupers in institutions instead;
- to reduce numbers of paupers applying for relief by making workhouse life so unpleasant for able-bodied paupers that "his situation, on the whole, shall not be made really or apparently so eligible as the situation of the independent labourer of the lowest class".

Dorset, contrary to the Poor Law Commissioners, set up a "General Mixed Workhouse" for the sick, aged, feeble-minded and orphaned. The same severe conditions were used for the able-bodied adults and vagrants. The workhouse avoided parish subsidies to labourers to support their family, children and aged parents. It was hoped that imprudent marriages to bring a subsidy for each child would be reduced. Mothers of bastards no longer enjoyed parish premiums for their error. Another anticipated side effect was the increase in wages for labourers by employers.

The main criticism in 1841 by the Poor Law Commissioners was the rigid separation of families, particularly elderly couples. From 1847 elderly couples were permitted to share a room by request. The workhouses represented a heavy investment (over £13 million between 1834 and 1883). A particular logic was developed. Their external walls shut out any view of the outside, a problem when educating the young who needed to be aware of what happened in the world around them. Private Charities were criticised for undermining the good work of the Poor Law.

There is no evidence of a poorhouse in Hooke, although it seems likely that there was one. There was a poorhouse at North Poorton (now a thatched cottage). It is possible that this also served Hooke, coming under the same part of the Manorial Court. One of the problems of the paternalism of the Poor Law at that time was that the gentry saw themselves as owners of the labourers. Any paternalism was in the mind rather than in fact in most parishes. The intention was to control and regulate with a general philosophy of "Don't tamper with the natural order." The basis of any education was to fit men for their earthly journey(!).

The parishes, including Hooke, were united for the administration of the relief of the poor in the name of the Beaminster Poor Law Union. Beaminster became head of a Union of twenty-six parishes for administering the workhouse for the poor. The Union Workhouse was completed in 1838 at Stoke Water (now private flats/apartments!). It is a Y-shaped building and provided accommodation for 230 persons. The Beaminster Poor Law Union population dropped significantly after 1841, partly caused by agricultural depression and partly by emigration. In 1850, according to the Half-Year Statement, there was one "indoor" male pauper resident from Hooke and 53 "outdoor" paupers "relieved" (out of the population of 268). In 1864 a vagrant's ward was erected to accommodate 16 men and 3 women. By 1912 the workhouse functioned mainly as an Infirmary.

Criminals and the police

The whole of the criminal reform legislation in the 19th century would have had an effect on a village like Hooke. The removal of gibbets, the pillory and the death sentence (now only for murderers), must have been a great relief to many poor agricultural workers who, not that many years before, could have been hanged for stealing an animal. There was no police force, only local constables who could be elderly and ineffective. The use of thief takers and a militia type constabulary would be unlikely in a village such as Hooke. The new laws introduced by Peel provided a professional police force for the first time. Hooke had its own Police Station from 1859-1886. It is clear that the policeman, who also served Rampisham and Wraxall, did not have a hectic life. The Police Station is now Ivy Cottage. The light outside is the original police light without the blue glass! The style is very similar to street lamps used in Broadwindsor (as in Beaminster Museum).

The village obviously had some characters. It is interesting to compare the fines and costs, some of which were quite severe for that time.

Extracts from the Police Beat Book: Hooke Police Station (1859-1886)

1859 William Forsey (labourer), one eye closed:
Stealing wood ... 2 months

1860 William Davey (labourer):
Profane swearing fined 10s, 10s costs.

1864 William Green (navvy), very abusive man:
Vagrancy ... 21 days.

1866 George Newman (butcher):
Horse straying fined 1s. (This was March 12)

1866 George Newman (butcher):
Horse straying fined 8s, 7s costs (April 28).

1868 Sarah Ann Daws (labourer):
Assault dismissed

1868 Sarah Legg (prostitute) (same date)
Assault fined 2s 6d

1869 William Cornick (unknown occupation) ... poacher? (*the question mark is in the record)*
Stealing 2 pheasants ... 2 months hard labour

1869 Robert Hallett (miller)
Donkey straying fined 10s

1876 Robert Hallett (miller's baker) (*the former miller)*
Selling bread without weights fined 10s.

1879 Edwin Hoddinott (dairyman)
Keeping dogs without licence fined 8s, 8s costs

1881 James Higgins (labourer)
Setting fire to a cottage. Acquitted at assizes; died.

The Criminal register for Dorset 1805-1840 shows a person by the name of Soloman Cornick from Hooke, who was imprisoned for 6 months for larceny in 1825. In 1835 a Reuben Cornick from Hooke was found not guilty of larceny. In 1836 Soloman Cornick reappeared on larceny charges and was given transportation for 7 years. There is no record of whether he was transported or to where.

Hooke wood/park was a popular area for poachers.

Need for bridges

Tragedies were not unusual. A Mr Hutchins (about 34 years old) was a carter at Toller Whelme. He lived at either Toller Whelme or Hooke. In 1895 he was taking a load of cow feed from Toller Porcorum station. He crossed the ford at Lower Kingcombe (some say Hooke, although this seems unlikely as there were bridges at Hooke by then). He was sitting on the shaft of the cart. He jumped off the shaft after crossing the stream and lost his footing, falling and both wheels of the wagon went over him. The lad accompanying him fetched Mr Wallbridge the farmer who happened to be close by but he was already dead. P. C. Pearce was soon on the scene and had the body removed. Hutchins left a wife and eight children. The coroner's report required Dorset County Council to improve the crossing. A similar accident had occurred two years previously when the Earl of Sandwich's carriage was upset and two of his servants were thrown into the stream.

William Mabey recalls the death of a boy who drowned whilst wading through the river on his way to Sunday School

Village outings

Judging by other villages there may well have been occasional outings, using horses and carts until such time as motorized charabancs became available. These outings may have been very local or even to places such as West Bay. There are certainly photographs of charabanc outings in the 1920s, although the actual dates are uncertain.

Leisure and sport

When Hooke Court was re-furbished as a shooting box Edward VIII, then Prince of Wales, came and stayed as a house-guest at Hooke Court. The visitors may well have been impressed by the landlord's generosity in rebuilding the village. It is reputed that Lily Langtree stayed in Juniper House during his visits. Other local stories suggest that she was in Hooke Court, presumably with the Prince of Wales, and had to climb out of the window on the side of the house facing the moat to avoid being discovered.

In 1896 the Earl of Sandwich had a nine-day shooting party that bagged 4237 pheasants and rabbits. There was, however, a shooting accident. Colonel Papillon was in a party cover shooting. He was on rising ground with Mr Colfox below. The Colonel went forward and his head came in the line of fire just as Mr Colfox shot a rabbit. One of the pellets entered the corner of his eye socket, passing out behind the nose, but happily missing the eye itself "and there is no reason for fearing any serious consequences"!

Transport routes

The tithe map of 1840 shows no road going across Warren Hill. However, the road was unfenced and would have counted as part of the land. It was the coach route through Hooke prior to the turnpike road. The coach (which was probably a fairly simple cart that took goods and people) went from Crewkerne to Beaminster and Maiden Newton.

Manorial Court Records

The Manorial Court records stopped in 1838. Only two families have attended as members of the court throughout the period 1708 to 1838: the Mintern(e)s and the Shorts. In 1828 a house called Hook House changed hands, having previously appeared on the roll in 1797. Was this Hooke Court or another house? In 1832 the buildings on Teavers Tenement were out of repair. Teavers Tenement does not appear on the tithe map so may have been in one of the other hamlets.

Hooke Population

Whilst Beaminster wages were higher than anywhere else in Dorset in 1831, the same was certainly not the case in Hooke. The Civil Division of the County of Dorset gave the following information for 1831:

Eggardon Hundred Divisions: Hooke and Witherston

County Rate: Annual Value of Real property	Amount of Poor's Rate raised	Amount of County Rate	Population
2771	125	19s 3d	269

The figures are as they appeared in the document and the rate had not changed since 1740.

In 1851 the list of important people was given as:

"Bartlett, Mr Theophilus
Wallis, Mr William

Coombs Chas, flax and tow spinner
Cram, Thomas, boot and shoemaker
Crofts, John, miller and baker
Holt, George, Farmer
Legg, Henry, farmer and carrier
Legg John, farmer
Legg, John, *Masons Arms* and carrier to Bridport, *Legg* sat. parish clerk, Knights-in-the-Bottom
Mintern, James and Samuel, farmers and grocers
Mintern, Jacob, baker and grocer
Rawlins, John and Davis, James, farmers
Silley John, gamekeeper
Studley, John, dairyman
Tompkins, Richard, dairyman.
Hooke, it had no charitable donations."

The population changes in Hooke are shown in the table below.

1801	1811	1821	1831	1841	1851	1861	1871	1881	1891	1901
184	206	234	269	268	261	247	202	154	179	155

In 1831 Hooke was stated to cover 1191 acres, have 51 houses inhabited (remarkably similar to the 55 in 2000), "55 families, 41 families employed in agriculture, 10 families employed in trades, manufacture and handicrafts, 4 other families. There were 120 males and 149 females. There were 53 males over 20 and 67 under 20. 3 labourers were employed by occupiers; 3 occupiers not employing labourers; 36 labourers employed in agriculture. 5 were employed in trade, handicraft as masters or workmen. There was 1 capitalist/banker/professional/educated. There were 4 labourers that were non-agricultural. There was 1 other."! There were 3 male servants under 20 and 8 female servants.

In 1915 the list of people in the village includes:

Samuel Loveridge, *Parish Clerk*
George Paull, *Sub-postmaster*
Miss Edith Boyd, *Schoolmistress*
Revd Richard Thomas Parker B. A., *Rector*
As well as:
Sandwich, Earl of, KCVO, JP.

Kelly's Directory also states:

"The village was served by the railways from Toller Station, on the Maiden Newton to Bridport branch line."

Agriculture

Tenant farmers and the steward

In 1841 the farmers are listed as George Holt, Henry Legg (also the carrier), and John Legg.

In 1876 George F Crocker took up the tenancy of Hooke Farm. He was required to pay 6% p.a. on the value of a new house to be built and 6.5% on extra drainage that was to be installed on the land, in addition to £713 annual rent. The house, the Bailiff's Cottage and Hill Cottage were in a poor state of repair. In the winter considerable damage occurred to the roof. The tenant asked for it to be repaired and was charged £269, which he considered high.

In the first summer rabbits and hares considerably damaged crops. When Mr Crocker complained, the steward Mr Peter Purves from Huntingdonshire pointed out that the landlord, the Earl of Sandwich, liked to have rabbits and hares on the estate. Presumably they were attractive for shooting.

There was an extensive exchange of correspondence over the next six years. One pair of letters relate to an attempt to charge Mr Crocker interest on the outlay for the new house *before* it was built. The new house did not materialise, but over £1000 was spent on extending the existing house, providing a bathroom with hot and cold water, and installing new fireplaces. There was a dispute over drainage. The steward insisted that the tenant had to provide cartage for the pipes. Stiles, fences and bridges had to be maintained by the tenant, but the materials were to be provided by the landlord, but none were provided. The limekilns on the farm were out of repair.

The tenant was given notice to quit. He claimed in 1881 for a series of recompenses amounting to £1000. The solicitor for the tenant suggested an out of court settlement but there was no reaction from the defendant's solicitor. In 1882 a writ was issued in the High Court of Justice, Queen's Bench division outlining similar requirements for payment. In the ensuing series of claims and counter claims it became clear that neither tenant nor landlord had any accounts, account books or receipts relating to the tenancy. The Master made an order referring the action to an official referee, but eventually the plaintiff got cold feet. The final solution was a payment of £150 with each paying their own costs!

This episode does little credit to the farmer or the vengeful incompetence of the steward. A new tenant in 1881 (Mr Little) paid £400 annual rent! The correspondence on his behalf mentions "the arable land is in a disgraceful state; all the wood wants painting and the door locks and windows repairing; the wet comes through the wall at the west end of the house in the bedroom and runs down into the room beneath.” There is also a request for “a stable, and a house for my trap and gates and bars repaired”. The agents, Symonds, describe it as “bleak situation, unfavourable distance from market towns, poor general condition of the farm, damage from the rabbits coming out of the woods”. In 1888 there was an agreement with Henry H Yeates for 288 acres the rent now down to £286 8s annually, payable in equal portions quarterly. He was required to keep in good order the house, gates, fences and mounds, to manage the land including laying dung, to maintain the ditches and hedges, drains and watercourses. He could rabbit with ferrets in hedgerows. The other game rights remained the landlord’s.

Mr Purves, the steward, seems to have had some odd ideas. When the plans for the new farm, now Manor Farm, were being developed, it was agreed that the homestead was ideal but a letter to Mr Purves from a Wm. Neale on April 2nd 1859 tactfully suggests that a barn and cattle yard would be a good idea! There was considerable discussion about the stones to be used with samples from Maiden Newton, Frome Vauchurch and later even a quarry at Hooke. However the final buildings include some beautifully built barns dated 1868 made in Bath stone and mudstone with tooled lintels and hand-made doorways. It almost looks as though it was originally designed for more opulent surroundings where it was not used and the materials were used instead at Hooke. There was also a massive land drainage scheme approved by the Land Drainage Board. Presumably these are the drains that still run down parallel to Green Lane, although much disturbed when the cottages were built in the middle of the village.

There were originally five builders interested in building the farm, but by a process of attrition the numbers come down to three, however one letter stated “I fear these builders will give us some trouble”. The eventual estimates were around £3600.

Farm labourers

The state of the peasantry was investigated on several occasions. In Somerset in 1846/7 examples were given in the *Bridgwater Times:*

“The almost entire failure of the potato in this parish and the potato being here the stuff of life to the working labourers, I fear the severest destitution and distress must be the result in the coming winter, from the low wages paid and the extreme high prices of all the necessities of life. The quarten loaf was charged 8d whilst in Bridgwater it was charged 7½d. Soap, candles etc. have during the past week risen one half penny a pound. Potatoes are 10s per bag and wheat is 8s or 9s per bushel … the wages in such a parish are 7s a week in Summer and 6s a week in Winter.”

“When he is able to work he gets about 6s a week, but suffers from bad health. He has a miserable mud dwelling, not yet completed on a corner piece of waste land from which he pays an acknowledgement of 1s per year to the lord of the manor. The roof of this dwelling is but slightly – ever so slightly – covered with straw, the walls are yet wet. The wall at the back of the house is not finished reaching only to about the height of the doorway. The remaining space to the roof is topped up with hay and rubbish. … The family never taste any meat.”

An article in *The Times*, Monday August 3rd 1846 states “There is also a parish called Hook, in the neighbourhood of Beaminster, to which my attention was directed since I left that town, and which I have since had an opportunity of visiting. The nature of distress which exists here will also justify a few remarks. The wages of the labourer here are the very lowest on which life can be supported, and the dwellings appropriated to him are, in most instances, absolutely ruinous and demand the assistance of props inside and out to keep them from the ground. I have some reason to suppose my arrival in the village was in some degree expected and prepared for. In the first house at which I applied for information, I found a young woman of about 20 or 21 years of age, and a child about eight years, the rest of the family being absent on their daily occupation. She informed me that she was the eldest daughter of the inmate of the cottage. I inquired what was the amount of her father's earnings. She 'did not know'. I next asked what rent they paid for the house. To this she pleaded ignorance. I then ventured to ask how many children her father had. She 'could not recollect'. But the child who was present, to the last query answered in an undertone 'six', for which she was immediately reprimanded and silenced. In general I have found throughout my inquiries no unwillingness to afford information. The labourer generally seems happy to have an opportunity of relating his grievances, and in general, I think, the chief thing to be guarded against is exaggeration. In the case I have just mentioned I feel little doubt but that strict injunctions of silence had been laid on this man and his family. I, however, discovered others whom want had rendered more communicative, and who afforded me long and minute accounts of distress and poverty. It is impossible to conceive the miserable state in which the inhabitants of this village pass their lives. They are the victims of every evil attendant upon want and insufficient lodging. The almost total absence of furniture is a conspicuous feature in this place. It generally consists of a couple of rough benches and a foundered table, the latter usually set against a wall in order to supply the deficiency of a leg."

In the seventeenth century labourers were paid 13d each day, 14d in the eighteenth century. The wages of a Dorset labourer in 1846 were 7s per week, although the last shilling was sometimes difficult to obtain! A bushel of grist, tailings or seconds was 7s. It would take 56 days to earn a quarter of grist.

Local effects of the changes in farming practices

After the early enclosure, the rapid changes in agriculture would have had some effect in Hooke. The introduction of drainage (Manor Farm depends on its land drains), fertilisers, mixing soils, new strains of cattle and sheep have had an effect since the nineteenth century leading to the rye-grass dominated pastures with silage as the modern farming equivalent of over-production.

The effect of the Napoleonic Wars at the end of the eighteenth century with the blockades put pressure on agriculture and caused increases in prices and increased production. In 1815 there was a crash in prices, also causing a collapse of wages and the associated poor housing of agricultural workers in Dorset that led to the Swing riots and the Tolpuddle Martyrs.

Up to the nineteenth century the water meadows would have been in regular use. The obvious remaining evidence is the field to the west of the church by the river. The ridges had channels in them from which a shallow rapidly-moving sheet of water flowed into the troughs protecting the land from frosts to give early grass for grazing. In other villages the water meadows were opened on March 25th, were watered again later in the year, used for hay rather than sheep, and closed in September. It seems rather strange that this should be the case as the original purpose was to provide early grazing.

Most farmers were tenants renting at the beginning of the 19th century. There was a price protection using tariffs for imports of corn (Corn Laws 1815). These laws were repealed in 1846. By the late 1870s the agricultural depression bit as grain was imported from USA, frozen meat from Argentina, Australia and New Zealand. The farm labourers had a terrible time throughout Victoria's reign living in appalling conditions with less and less work as the century came to an end. The population of Hooke had already started to decline and continued to do so until the late 20th century.

The tithe map of 1840 estimated that the parish was 1190 acres: 20 acres arable, 502 acres of meadow or pasture, 6 acres of gardens and orchard land, 5 acres of woodland (the larger woods seem to have been omitted). There was 36 acres of glebe land. However Hoe Barton (now called Hooke Farm) had coppices at Park Westcombe, Horsemoor and Coppice Castle and paid "customary payments of £2 13s 4d and in addition 1s for every milch cow and 8d for every heifer kept and depastured in lieu of tithes on the milk". The arable crops were about 47 bushels of wheat, value 7s 11¼d; barley 83.6 bushels, value 3s 11½d; oats 120 bushels, value 2s 9d.

The ownership of some of the properties and land was with the Pope family: John Pope, Benjamin and Thomas, all of Toller Whelme.

Mechanisation had an impact in Dorset farms in 1840s, requiring fewer workers. Horse-powered threshing machines were replaced by a steam-driven ones. By 1853 there were 16 steam engines on Dorset farms. These engines carried out the following functions: threshing, straw shaking, winnowing, sacking, and straw into chaff, propelling the grain into a dry covered shed. From 1879, a bad summer, there was a depression in farming that lasted almost unchecked until 1940.

The land in Hooke was principally dairy land in the 19th century. In 1915 Kelly's Directory gives the chief crops as: oats, barley and roots, but the land was principally pasture.

Woodland

There are several stands of Scots pine. It is claimed in one publication (Dorset Countryside Treasures in W. Dorset Part 1) that these are part of "extensive 19th century planting of shelter belts". A more likely explanation is that they were planted in the 19th century as "eye-catchers" to define or mark out the boundary of an estate and as a quick source of building material.

Oak wood began to rise in price rapidly from about 1820 because of the value of the bark for tanning. The underwood of oak was maintained at the expense of timber because of the needs of the tanning trade. It is possible that the two oak coppices became mainly sources of charcoal and bark for tanning. Certainly there were still several limekilns including a large one by the chalk pit below Westcombe Coppice. The bottom fell out of the oak sales for shipbuilding and tannery in about 1850. Coal usually would have replaced charcoal for lime kilns but this was unlikely at Hooke because the nearest railway station was at Toller Porcorum with a tortuous journey to the kilns. The two oak coppices appear to have been planted more recently than this date, perhaps at the time it was fashionable to plant oak woods.

At some time after the Tithe Map of 1840 the pastureland shown between Hooke Park and the old Dorset Ridgway was planted with trees.

Water sources and water cress

There are at least three dewponds at the top end of Green Lane. These are typical sites on the chalk. The technique of generating a dewpond was to use or make a depression that was lined with puddled clay, filled by rainfall and runoff from the surrounding slopes with some assistance from the mist. There were problems in choosing sites and also preventing animals from putting their hooves in and damaging the clay lining. Two of the dewponds are on the left near the top of Green Lane, one now full of small trees, and one on the corner of Green Lane and Warren Hill that still holds some water. The owner has made some efforts to keep the latter relatively clear of trees.

Watercress started to be grown commercially in about 1900. Watercress requires an abundance of water and the chalk streams of Dorset provide an ideal environment with a water temperature of about 52^{0}F all year. A healthy stock was maintained by frequent clearing and replanting of beds. The best planting period was the winter. Topping occurred from June to September. Seeds were sown from April to August, after 6 weeks the plants had developed enough to handle. Tufts of seedlings (pullings) were removed to other beds. Several thinnings occurred before the plants were left to flower. As the beds flowered the watercress was scythed and the flowers discarded. The crop was cut in the late summer and pulled in winter. It was cleaned, bundled, pushed into cartons and cooled (about 34^{0}F for 20 minutes). It was despatched over night. The watercress was taken by cart to Toller Porcorum to go by train to London. Hooke watercress is thought to have been served at the Ritz.

The carter is reputed to have been interested in the postmistress and would leave his cart outside the post office with a nosebag on the horse for it to feed. On one occasion the old horse died whilst the carter was in the post office. There is no information about whether the watercress got to London on time or whether his employers took any action!

Photographs

The following photographs show how Hooke used to be.
The photographs are mainly shown in chronological order.
Most of the photographs relate to information that has been given in Chapters 7-9.

Hooke Church 1870
Hooke Church 1900

The Earl of Sandwich and the Prince of Wales at Hooke Court 1888
Shooting Party at Hooke in 1888

Charabanc outing
Cottages by the lake

Hooke School 1937
Skittles in the Glebe Field

Horse being shod at the Forge
Mr Drewett's fruit delivery

Hooke Court about 1935
Hooke Home Guard

Hunt's ice cream van at St. Francis' School
Outdoor P. E. at St. Francis' School

Park Pond in about 1970
Watercress beds

Mill in about 1970
Mill in 2000

Mintern table tomb
Inscription on the gravestone of The Reverend J Penrose and Mrs L Penrose.

Hooke Church 1870 (photograph by Richard Hine of Beaminster)
Showing the remnants of the leat, note also the stairs to the gallery by the tower stump.

Hooke Church 1900 (photograph by Richard Hine of Beaminster)
Note the tall chimney on the tower for the heating.

The Earl of Sandwich and The Prince of Wales
at Hooke Court in about 1888.

Shooting Party at Hooke in 1888
The Earl of Sandwich is second from the left at the back.

Charabanc Outing from Hooke
Probably late 1920s for a trip to either to Weston-super-Mare or Weymouth.

Cottages by the current lake
Taken about 1930, showing Brook Cottages at their original height on the left, the cottage where the boy fell through the roof in the middle (now only a small section of wall by the road can be seen); St. Francis Cottage with lime wash for waterproofing, since removed with problems of water ingression. Note the 10 people standing in the road, all in their Sunday best!

Hooke School 1937

Skittles in the Glebe Field
In the 1930s with the Rectory in the background.

Horse being shod at the Forge
Note the tall chimney and the telephone kiosk.
The blacksmith is Mr Paull in about 1937.

Mr Drewett's Fruit Delivery
Mr Drewett later came to live in Hooke taking over the Paulet Arms.

Hooke Court about 1935

Hooke Home Guard
During World War II (shooting the instructor?)

Hunt's Ice Cream van at St. Francis School

Outdoor PE at St. Francis School
Note the East wing of Hooke Court before demolition.

Park Pond in about 1970

Watercress beds
Where the current lake is, looking towards Juniper House and Hooke Court.

Mill in about 1970

Mill in 2000

Minterne table tomb in Hooke churchyard

Inscription on gravestone of The Reverend J. and Mrs. L. Penrose in Hooke churchyard.

Chapter 8

The Salts
(1917-1947)

National Background and Village Structure

Nationally

King George V's reign continued for the beginning of this phase of Hooke's history. The Great War ended in 1918 and was followed by troubled times. The problems in Ireland caused the 1920 partition of Ireland. Industrial problems came to a head with the 1926 General Strike following the first Socialist government of 1924. The world economic crisis of 1929-1931 had implications for everyone in Britain. In 1931 the king persuaded the three political parties to form a National Government. On his death his son Edward VIII became king from January 20th 1936, but was not crowned before he abdicated on December 11th 1936, to be succeeded by his brother king George VI. The Second World War started in 1939, during which the king visited the front line. The end of the war in Europe was in 1945 and in the Far East in 1946. He and his queen, Elizabeth, had close contact with the people. 1945 saw the beginnings of nationalisation.

Church

The last rector, the Reverend T Parker, died on March 24th 1939 aged 90. When he was in his 90s his housekeeper used to read his sermons in church. He lost a son, Lance Corporal John Parker of the Dorsetshire Regiment, in the First World War (a copy of the citation is shown on the next page) and there are memorial plaques to both of them in the church. The son's memorial in the church states "In loving memory of John F Parker son of the present rector who died for his country on April 4 1918. AET23". The Parker grave is on the South side of the church near to Rampisham Hill. The Rectory was sold in 1939, but as a condition of the sale was not allowed to be called rectory, presbytery, parsonage or any other similar name. It is currently called Hooke House.

The gate into the churchyard from Higher Street Lane had a simple iron arch with an oil lamp in a glass container. Possibly the structure was made by the local blacksmith. The arch and the glass were blown down in a gale in about 1941. The capping stones on the gate pillars still have the metal in their centres from this arch.

Heating was installed in the church in about 1951. The roof and windows were repaired in 1952, the same year that the Reverend G White, joint vicar of Toller Porcorum and Hooke, died (on January 27th).

Hooke Court and the Village

In 1919 Samuel P Mintern had his will proved in the Supreme Court of Queensland, Australia. He left £6 0s 9d for the benefit of the poor inhabitants of Hooke. His father had probably dropped the 'e' from the surname. The Mintern Trust still exists today and has a healthy sum of money, although there are few poor to benefit.

In 1919 Hooke Court was sold by the Duke of Cleveland and the Earl of Sandwich to Sir Thomas Salt.

HE whom this scroll commemorates was numbered among those who, at the call of King and Country, left all that was dear to them, endured hardness, faced danger, and finally passed out of the sight of men by the path of duty and self-sacrifice, giving up their own lives that others might live in freedom.

Let those who come after see to it that his name be not forgotten.

L/Cpl. John Parker
Dorsetshire Regt.

Descriptions of Hooke village in the inter-war years are that "it is scattered along the hillside following the course of the little river, a place of plain cottages, an old-fashioned village shop and Post Office and a modest inn. By the late 1930s there was also a telephone kiosk outside the post office, brought by horse and cart. The church is much restored but has retained some fifteenth century work in the panelled arch in the south chapel and a hexagonal font of the same period. The roads here are narrow, twisty, steep banked and often surprisingly wet. The wild, well-wooded country of Hooke Park and the Forestry Commission is virtually unknown and there is nothing 'tourist' in the accepted sense of the word."

Other buildings in the village

The old cottages near the mill (now called Brook Cottages) were single storey with a thatched roof. Much of the work in extending to two stories was carried out during WWII by Crowes the builders for Mrs Goddard, the watercress farm owner. She also bought Hooke Court when the Salts sold it, but she soon sold it to the Franciscan Brothers.

There was reputed to be a small mill where the house called Kingfishers now stands or behind the present site. There were previously two or three terraced thatched cottages there. One report suggests that this was a fulling mill, although a small gristmill seems more likely.

The pub in the village, the Paulet Arms, was well frequented by farmers. They would have had their horse and cart parked outside, come out the worse for wear and the horse would take them home.

The village school had two entrances, one for boys and one for girls. There were two classrooms. The teacher lived in a house attached to the school. The old school bell has recently been returned to its home to hang outside Old School House.

The village in the late 1930s as recalled by Mr Hillman

The following are the recollections when he lived in the village as a 10-year old boy.

"Just before the Second World War any person employed at Hooke Court lived in a tied cottage. When that person became ill he had to leave. It was a closed village with little contact with the outside world. The horizon was its limits, although walks to Beaminster and Toller Porcorum occurred. There was an occasional charabanc outing to Weymouth.

"The school took from infants to age 14. Girls went into service and boys into farming (so little had changed since Thomas Hardy's time). The pupils were from the surrounding farms and the village. There was a bell in a little belfry above the cloakroom (the bell now hangs outside The Old School House). The current garden was the playground. On the wall of the schoolroom was a picture of Sir Francis Drake as a young man with an old mariner pointing to sea. The picture inspired at least one former pupil to join the Royal Navy. Mrs Clegg was the schoolmistress (Mr Clegg worked at Westlands) and they had a bull-nosed Morris with a noisy engine that you could hear in the village as it climbed Chalk Hill. Mrs Clegg was tolerant, but if you had stolen something she would find out. There was a pecking order at school: farmers' sons, persons who sold goods from emerging new industries (e.g. radios, vacuum cleaners – a special mystique amongst the community) were highest and labourers' sons were bottom … feudal. The Clegg's son loved oranges that were quite a luxury. There were two other teachers, one of whom had a bun, wore pince-nez and rode a daisy bicycle. The school was the centre of village social life. There was a large fire and country dancing was held there led by a man playing a Melodium and a violin.

The first villager to have a private car lived at Church Cottages. The car was a £100 Ford. Everybody else walked or cycled."

There is still a large oak tree near to the entrance of Manor Farm. It was there in 1937 and seemed as large as it is now. As a boy he used to climb it and play in it. He also remembered playing on the green in the river near the bridge at Toller.

Manor Farm belonged to the Wallbridges. As a boy, when his Dad was ill, Mrs Wallbridge was very kind. He used to saw logs and play on the swing in the garden. The labourers used to come to breakfast in the kitchen of the farm that had a flagstone floor. The milkmaids went with their yolks and buckets to fetch water from the large well behind The Buildings to the farm. In 1937 a rotary hand pump was installed in a shed making the drawing of water much easier. Looking up beyond Manor Farm was a clump of trees where the cowman could be seen and heard singing songs of the day.

"The occupants of The Buildings (from the top house) were a worker on the estate who died, somebody who has been forgotten, my father (he was a handyman at Hooke Court) who had a wireless pole in the garden and a radio, and the Kings – he was a Dorset County Council employee who looked after the hedges and ditches. The field behind was well maintained with a clear view. There was a path to The Court. There was a hayrick that used to smoke (steam). Up to the left there used to be shooting, and picnics were held at the top. Hazel nuts were picked and eaten. Hazel pipes were made from the branches. A walk to Knights-in-the-Bottom could result in the loss of Wellingtons in the bog and difficulty in extracting oneself. There were wild irises and orchids there (unfortunately lost in the developments that have taken place there)." He loved running down Green Lane and also riding down on his Fairey bicycle; he tried in it on ice on one occasion and almost had a nasty accident. The gardens on the left (half way from The Buildings to Church Cottages) were all vegetable gardens. Most people were self-sufficient because they had small incomes.

"The Salts were kind and benevolent, strict and somewhat despotic. People were paid by cheque and there was no rent for cottages. The labourers were paid about 3s each week! Where the bungalows are now near the green (*one has since been made into two storeys*) were three labourers' cottages. The Salts were good to their tenants and workers. There was a picture of Miss Patricia presented by The Court to each cottage and everybody was given presents at Christmas. Lady Salt was a patron of the school and sold National Savings stamps. Patricia Salt's husband-to-be flew over the village in a brand new Air Force biplane doing aerobatics and dropped a note on the lawn of Hooke Court for her.

"The Court seemed massive. It was said that the Salts made their money from tea and investments in Argentina (*they were bankers*). They were abroad a lot. They had a retinue of servants: a cook (Swedish), other cooks, a butler in uniform and other butlers (*presumably footmen*), gardeners and handymen. There were electric lights (d. c. with batteries) driven by a Rustin Hornsby gas engine. There were central heating radiators; they had their own drainage and hydraulic rams for water. They had their own petrol pump. There were Hunt Balls for the Cattistock Hunt. There were parties with marquees and all the estate workers were sometimes invited."

The church seemed enormous to a small boy. There was a choir that sat in the south aisle. "The organ was played by Mrs. Parker. The rector was Reverend Parker who stuttered. Mrs. Parker held Sunday School in the rectory. If you attended Sunday School regularly you were given a hymnbook and a bible. When Mrs Parker died the entire village were outside the church and stood around the grave. The bell was tolled for each year of life of the deceased.

It was quite an event. There were laurel trees behind the wall by the road.

"The blacksmith, husband of the shop owner, was also the undertaker. Shire horses were shod. The yard was used for sweating on iron tyres to wheels. It was also where the coffins were made. His wife ran the shop where you bought sweets. The Paulls were both nice. You could get anything at the shop and it was a sort of village forum. There was a telephone kiosk outside that was delivered by a horse and cart. The pole for the two wires was along from the churchyard (there is still a pole there now). There was a hole dug for the pole and enormous blocks to support the hawser. The doctor used a room at the post office for his visits.

"The postman cycled from Beaminster. He had a peak at the front and at the back of his cap. The Paulet Arms was a Devenish pub and was frequented mainly by waggoners and farm labourers."

The consumption of tobacco went from £40M in 1914 to £204M in 1939 and £564M in 1945. By 1948 80% of men and 40% of women bought cigarettes and smoked about 12 each day. Meanwhile the consumption of beer fell. In 1910-13 the consumption was 34M barrels, which fell to about 17M barrels in the 1930s. The amount of drunkenness fell, possibly also due to the reduction in the gravity of the beer associated with a large rise in price. It is noticeable that the publicans in Hooke had a separate employment as well.

"One of the events in the village was when the road was tarred. A steamroller would arrive after tar barrels were placed along the road at intervals. The steamroller, pulling a caravan and water carrier, was parked outside the rectory opposite the school. The steamroller driver was a source of adulation. He banked his fire at night. There was a horse drawn tar pot with two men: one pumped the tar, the other spread it and both were covered in tar. The grit was from another horse drawn lorry." After Sunday School one day, in his best clothes, he went to one of the tar barrels just beyond Bridge Farm. It was a very hot day and the bung was on the bottom side of the barrel and was leaking. Intrigued, he pulled it out: tar all over the road and on his Sunday best: he was not the most popular person with his mother!

"The Goddards came from Frampton and lived at Hooke Farm that was run as a watercress farm. He was a big fellow. He had a daughter Mary and several other children. Mr. Goddard had a car, a sort of Al Capone type car. Villagers helped on the farm packing watercress. They often had breakfast with the Goddards; Mrs Goddard was very nice. Juniper House was then called Home Farm. The mill was still used to grind corn; the tall end was where the grain was lifted up. The wheel was driven from a leat coming from the direction of the watercress beds.

"There was a public notice board outside what are now Brook Cottages. It gave notices of typhoid outbreaks in London! The butler lived in what is now St. Francis Cottage; he was a big noise in the village. Next door (towards the church) was a thatched cottage in poor condition. An investigation by a small boy including climbing on the roof resulted in falling into the cottage (*presumably unoccupied*)."

Hospitals became universal with special provision for the poor. The nearest was at Bridport, so people from Hooke now had better care when very ill.

"The Salt family sold the 240 acres of Hooke Park to the Unigate Pension Fund during the Second World War."

Friends of a small boy were cows, horses, and cats rather than just people. Seasons were part of life. Moving into an urban area needed a conversion course! He joined the Royal Navy and became a Stoker Mechanician, later transferring to the Medical Branch and becoming an instructor. He enjoyed teaching so much that he took his discharge and trained as a maths teacher and then took a degree course. He enjoyed his career as a teacher.

Individuals of Interest

Sir Thomas Salt was a Liberal politician and had his own bank in Stafford (the connection again). The bank was eventually sold to Lloyds Bank. There was a family connection to Wiggins the goldsmiths who became more well-known for electro-plated nickel silver, being ultimately bought out by Guest Keen and Nettlefold.

Extracts from Lady Elinor Salt's Diary (1920-1930)

According to the diary of Lady Salt they looked at Hooke Court on April 20th 1920. They arrived on July 19th by train with 21 packages and a bicycle. They met the bailiff, Higgins; the Rector and Mrs Parker called on the Salts, as did Mrs Buck.

A trout was introduced into the moat on August 7th. They were keen cyclists, cycling to Maiden Newton on August 26th and to Dorchester to get an ambulance for "old Isaacs" who had injured his back. On September 11th the Salts and the Parkers had a picnic for 11 by the moat. August 23rd 40 Dorset Horns were purchased. By October Lady Salt was helping Mrs Parker with Sunday School. In November the rose garden was planned and planted. On December 20th 1920 they visited all the cottages with crackers for the children. There was a Christmas tree for the village children. 48 came for tea, getting crackers, games, a bag of sweets, an orange and a sugar stick.

On January 14th 1921 the Salts called on the Wallbridges for tea. The Wallbridges at this time lived at Manor Farm. Lady Salt tried to get a District Nurse for the village, but the decision was postponed for 3 months. Kelly was "viewed" for the chauffeur's post. On March 31st there was a Sunday School tea and a Parish Social Evening and on April 7th some of the village (the Salts and 9 others) went on a charabanc outing to a Beaminster entertainment, the Hardy Players doing scenes from *Far from the Madding Crowd.* A presentation was made to Mrs Parker on April 12th to mark her playing of the "church organ" for 15 years. It is not clear whether there was a pipe organ at this time or a harmonium.

When the Parkers were away in June, the vicar of Melplash took a 3 p.m. service at Hooke. By June Lady Salt was helping with setting up the Brownies. On August 18th 12 Brownies were enrolled by Lady Digby in the billiard room at Hooke Court with "Mrs Parker, Peggy and Miss Martin". In September Miss Allen and little girls moved into the Lodge.

The architect, Captain Pike, on September 29th had identified repairs needed to the floors (already carried out on October 3rd) and a girder to strengthen the drawing room ceiling. Their furniture replaced the rented furniture at Hooke Court, rented from Captain Harverd. The furniture vans (with 13 men) arrived on October 7th. Servants were interviewed from October 19th-21st.

November saw the Brownies rehearsing a play to raise funds for Brownie uniforms and in December the older girls had a rehearsal of "Joy symphony". Again there were visits to all the village cottages with presents. *(Visits to cottages continued throughout the time that the Salts lived in Hooke and is verified by villagers who lived there at the time.)* The Christmas party was held in an empty cottage for 44 children with "Tommy" (aged 16) dressed as Father Christmas.

Obviously the interviews for servants had not been very successful because in February 1922 there was a visit to London to look for servants, some being interviewed at Harrods. Harding arrived on March 1st as a result of this foray.

Mrs Paull at the Post Office was visited on March 18th 1922; a day after her baby was born.

On June 15th "Evelyn" entertained the Parochial Church Council to tea, bowls and clock golf. On July 8th there was a tremendous storm with high winds. The Hooke Fete and Bazaar on September 8th raised £74.

In 1923 the moat was stocked with 100 5-inch long trout. On April 3rd there was an Easter Egg Hunt for the village, followed by a village concert on April 23rd. Cricket was flourishing with a match against Chedington on August 4th. On October 14th a farewell visit was paid to the village. All the servants left on October 17th. The Salts left for France and Majorca for the winter, returning to Hooke on June 13th 1924.

There were regular elections, one occurring in 1924, when the village had to go to Powerstock to vote. It would appear that the Salts helped with transport. The new cook, "most disagreeable", was replaced by Mrs Grey in November. The Christmas presents were distributed on December 24th.

By January 2nd 1925 there were bad floods, so that a trip to Dorchester was only just possible. On January 19th Lady Salt went to Dorchester to get a Driving Licence, having been driving since 1920. A Children's Library is mentioned on March 11th. On April 7th was the first meeting of the Hooke Women's Institute when Lady Salt was elected president. W.I. meetings and school managers' meetings feature regularly in the diary from then onwards. On September 17th 1925 Hobbs and other cricketers were in Bridport. On December 28th there was a party in the school attended by 90 children, mothers and babies.

January 16th 1926 saw very heavy snowfalls. On February 15th the Salts went to look at some electric lighting and Captain Pike came for lunch on April 18th to discuss this lighting. On May 4th the General Strike began and it prevented the Salts from going to Mrs Horner's 96th Birthday because of petrol shortages.

Each year Empire Day was celebrated in the school with flags, songs and dancing.

May 21st Elsie Kelly was not very well, possibly from consumption. On June 1st Captain Pike came to make final arrangements for fitting electric lights. On June 2nd the Salts left for Switzerland for a 3-week holiday. On returning they found the house in a terrible mess with the lighting being installed. July 12th Elsie Kelly died and was buried in Hooke Churchyard on July 16th. The Salts stayed at the Antelope Hotel in Dorchester whilst the work was finished. On September 13th the moat was partially drained. On December 24th presents were distributed around the village. By December 27th there was deep snow with drifts causing the school party on December 28th to be postponed because there were no deliveries, the only way out of Hooke was via Crocker's farm to Toller. The roads were still blocked in spite of rain.

Again there were still deep snow drifts on January 4th 1928, although it was finally possible to drive to Dorchester. By this time their daughter, Patience, now in her 20s, was helping with Brownies and Guides. On March 12th Lady Salt went to the Girl Guide Commissioners'

Conference (*presumably a Commissioner herself*) in London and was introduced to the Duchess of York (*the future Queen Elizabeth*). May 28th 1928 there was an expected tidal wave that could have submerged Weymouth and possibly the South of England ... "but it did not happen!"

Obviously the installation of a lavatory was quite an event as it occupied entries in the diary for the two weeks on returning from a French holiday in July, along with all the doors in the house being stained. In August the butler put a cartilage out in his knee, but Dr Hare put it back. On August 29th their son, George, bought a second hand car, a Clyno, for £65. On August 31st Patience had driving lesson in the Austin 7 with Kelly, the chauffeur. In September their other daughter, Patricia, was also involved with the Brownies, helping take them to the Brownie Revels in Maiden Newton. On October 8th Hanna Dish walked in her sleep and jumped out of a window. She broke her toes and had to be taken to Dorchester Hospital; by October 20th she was still in hospital and had had her toes set again. On November 16th there was a terrific gale and trees were down, so that a return journey from Dorchester had to be via Cerne Abbas. There were further gales on November 25th. December 1st saw Lady Salt's first visit to "talkie films – they were quite marvellous". December 4th King was very ill. December 24th the presents were taken round the village.

From 11th to 21st February 1929 there were blizzards in Dorset and skating was still possible in March. On 27th April Kelly, the chauffeur was taken ill early in the morning (a heart attack?) and had a second attack and died at about 12 noon. "Terrible shock to all: such a faithful friend and valuable servant". He was buried on May 1st in Hooke churchyard. The family were vaccinated for smallpox on May 4th (because there was an outbreak in Sherborne) and half of the household on May 10th. A temporary chauffeur, Worley, was on trial from May 8th, but another potential chauffeur Wood was interviewed on May 21st.

On June 27th Patience was presented at Court and Lady Salt and Patience dressed up in their court clothes to show the servants and their wives on June 29th. "Farm stealers" caught in the Park came to Petty sessions on July 29th and the case was dismissed. On September 14th Gay came for the day and 35lb. of blackberries were picked for her to take home. By July 28th they were getting anxious for the water supply (*so presumably there had been a long dry spell)* but it rained on "at last" September 29th. November 11th sloes were collected for sloe gin. December 5th saw heavy rain and gales with 14 trees down in Hooke, followed by further gales the next day and more trees down. December 24th the presents were taken round to the cottages.

At the W. I. meeting on January 6th 1930 nobody was willing to serve on the committee (*not only a recent phenomenon*) so the W. I. was disbanded for 9 months and no further mention is made during the diary in 1930. On January 12th there was a terrible gale that blew down the garden wall and many trees. March 13th, Mrs Coleman resigned as the teacher "very sorry". November 9th Lady Salt took 4 Guides and 6 Brownies to the Armistice service at Toller.

Interactions affecting people in the village

First World War

The Great War of 1914-18 had an impact throughout the country. There was a squadron of Blimps (small airships) based in Hooke Park that flew out over the channel and patrolled the coast during the day, returning at night. They were moored to cut-off tree trunks and were almost out of sight.

In the First World War conscription was imposed and agricultural workers probably passed the medical better than many city workers. The memorial in the church lists men from the village who lost their lives and also men who served in the armed services. The rector's son is included in the list in addition to his memorial tablet in the church.

Between the wars

Between the wars villagers would have joined the large crowds that went to see the Flying Circus in the field between Pipsford and the B-road to Beaminster. Bi-planes would race across the countryside from place to place. They would land in the field, called Racing Ground. One of their favourite tricks was to bomb Beaminster with flowers.

Second World War

The pikes that had been brought out to repel the Armada and Napoleon came into action again! There were insufficient rifles for the home guard in 1940 after Dunkirk so the pikes were rescued from the museums to be given to the Home Guard to repel the parachutists! Hooke had its own Home Guard and one photograph shows them learning to fire a rifle: all pointing at the instructor!

There were bombs dropped around Hooke in the Second World War. It is not clear whether they were aimed at the Rampisham masts or whether they were excess left over from raids on Swansea. One landed near the church and replacement panes of glass can be seen in the cathedral glass windows where the yellow edges are replaced with clear glass. A series of bombs landed parallel with the masts, one in Parsonage Coppice (the bomb crater is in the grubbed out field), one on the edge of the field where there is a cattle drinking trough and two more in the neighbouring parish (one of which is reputed to be unexploded).

In the Second World War there were no war-related deaths among residents of Hooke, although a former resident died whilst serving in the RAF. The son of the Goddards who ran the watercress farm was killed. He is given no specific place of residence in any records, so presumably had already left home at Hooke when he joined the RAF. He was a Flight Sergeant Pilot in 619 Squadron, Royal Air Force Volunteer Reserve. He appears to have been shot down over Germany on Monday September 6th 1943 and is buried at the Rheinberg War Cemetry, Kamp Lintfort, Nordhein-Westfal, Germany.

Brook Cottages were rebuilt during World War II by Mrs Goddard, raising the roof level from a thatched roof to the current slate roof. The old roofline can be seen on the end gable.

Agriculture

The water meadows would have become too expensive by the early or middle 20th century. The obvious water meadow by the church is now regularly ploughed and planted with rye grass. The hedgerows would have begun to change over the period from 1870. From 1870 to about 1950 was a period of agricultural adversity and the maintenance of hedgerows would have declined allowing unchecked growth.

After the First World War

Immediately after the war was one of the more prosperous times for agriculture. There were guaranteed prices for cereals, milk and potatoes. There were fixed minimum wages for labourers. Many women served in the fields and the cowsheds. Their pay was probably better than before the war and they could afford make-up that had become more common.

After the war there was a large reduction of women working in domestic service. Other occupations in towns and cities paid more. The first attempts at welfare were also introduced, eventually causing the closure of the workhouses.

By 1924 the economy had deteriorated and there were many unemployed. The state of agriculture was also somewhat parlous, more machinery becoming common and there was less need for labour, so the rural population continued to diminish. Agricultural wages were £82 for a year in 1924, £89 in 1935, despite the rise in the cost of living. Many lived in 'primary poverty' or 'utter destitution'.

By the 1930s further mechanisation had occurred with the advent of tractors and hay sweeps. The use of hand built stooks of corn was still occurring. However tractors were unreliable so there was not much incentive to invest in machinery! Increasing quantities of cheap imported foodstuffs were available. Wages were lower, arable farming was reduced and there was more concentration on milk, poultry, eggs and pigs. The advent of the Milk Marketing Board in 1933 at least brought regulated quantity, cleanliness and bonuses for TB-free herds. Milking machines were also available in the 1930s but were unreliable and required regular replacements. Hand milking was still the order of the day in Hooke until after the Second World War.

Second World War

The Second World War revolutionised farming with the need for home-grown foodstuffs supported by lots of incentives from government. Controls were put on sales and prices by the various marketing boards. There were: subsidies, incentive schemes, and quotas. There was assistance for mechanisation including combine harvesters, grain driers, milking machines, electric fencing and machines for silage making, hay making, straw baling. The milking machines in the Hooke valley had to wait for the advent of electricity into the valley after the war. There was much ploughing of land, including land in Hooke. Flax growing was encouraged to supply Fontmell industries mill at Netherbury. The main need was for fire hoses. The Women's Land Army from the Beaminster hostel provided much of the female labour including that needed in Hooke. The number of horses used had dropped dramatically whilst the number of tractors had increased, now that the use of rubber tyres with deep treads had replaced the steel lugs that were forbidden on public roads.

Sheep farming, the long time staple basis of Dorset farming, had declined. However sheep had never been the mainstay in Hooke.

Fallow deer were and still are probably more common than at any previous time. Many escaped from parks in the early 20th century. There was still a deer park in the time of the Salts in the 20th century. The deer had more opportunity to hide from humans, because there were so few workers on the land.

Watercress Farm

The valley with 16 springs became a watercress farm. It is understood that the beds here and above Juniper House may have been dug out by prisoners of war. Some of the watercress beds were named after first war battles such as the Somme. By the later years of the watercress farm there was a drip feed of chemicals into the beds. Seed was sold to other watercress farms at £1 per lb after the Second World War. When the ponds at the top were released from time to time there were eels and trout there.

Not only was the watercress sent to Covent Garden in London, but also sold to restaurants in London such as the Ritz. The watercress went from Toller Porcorum Station to London and the Midlands.

Kent growers were provided with wooden boxes sent from the timber mill at Toller Porcorum that also produced pit props. Did the timber originate from trees at Hooke? Certainly the mill dealt with timber from the felling in Hooke Park in the First and Second World Wars.

Woodland

Hooke Park is supposed to have been felled in the First World War, although this seems to conflict with the use of the woodland for hiding blimps. Any felled trees would have been taken to the sawmills at Toller Porcorum. Extensive felling occurred again during the Second World War, the trees being taken to Toller for the sawmill.

Chapter 9

Modern Times: The Estate Broken Up (1947-2000)

National Background and Village Structure

Nationally

King George VI died in 1952, to be succeeded by his daughter Elizabeth. The hallmarks of the present era seem to be Cold Wars, various other wars all over the world, some involving the UK and USA, a materialistic society and a compensation-ridden culture.

Hooke Village

After the war the village shop and Post Office was open at all hours, a knock at the door and Mrs Wrixon (who was Swedish) would provide! Mr Wrixon did all the hedges and ditches. The forge next door was used by Mr Leaf and his son who came two or three times each week until about 1952. Not only were the village horses shod but also the Cattistock Hunt horses.

Mrs Goddard sold Hooke Court to the Anglican Friars from Hillfield. They set up a boarding school for boys with emotional and behavioural difficulties (to use modern jargon) ... for "naughty boys" as far as the villagers were concerned. Dr Dearlove, the doctor came to the village each week to see the villagers and the boys.

Pines the Grocers called weekly for orders and delivered on a Saturday, the baker called several times each week and the butcher came weekly. Hunts Ice Cream came twice weekly, a special treat for the boys. The postmen came on motorbikes and delivered twice each day.

There was no triangle at the road junction near the church. The grass grew where no traffic ever went! "At the time of writing this area is less developed and up-to-date than almost any other part of Dorset which I can think of. This tumbled watershed bright with springs" (Hutchings 1967).

Some interesting comments written about Hooke in 1984 include:

"By the middle of the 20th century the mill had degenerated into a seedy cottage, but in 1969 it was acquired for restoration as a better-class residence. Today Hooke is a sequestered part of the world, and Hooke is a dying village though the agricultural land in the area is well maintained.

"Hooke Court, further down the hillside now belongs to the Brotherhood of St. Francis, well known for their work with boys in need of extra care. The school is a sunny looking building, in warm Ham-stone, with many Elizabethan touches in gable and window, with some good new building essential to the project's development, sitting oddly among the beeches."

The main mill ceased to function before 1940, the last wheel having been made in 1875. There were cottages on the west side of Green Lane and along Back Lane. There was a mill where Kingfishers bungalow now is and the river had been diverted. It would seem that the original path of the river is where the stream goes under the road before Bridge Farm. The

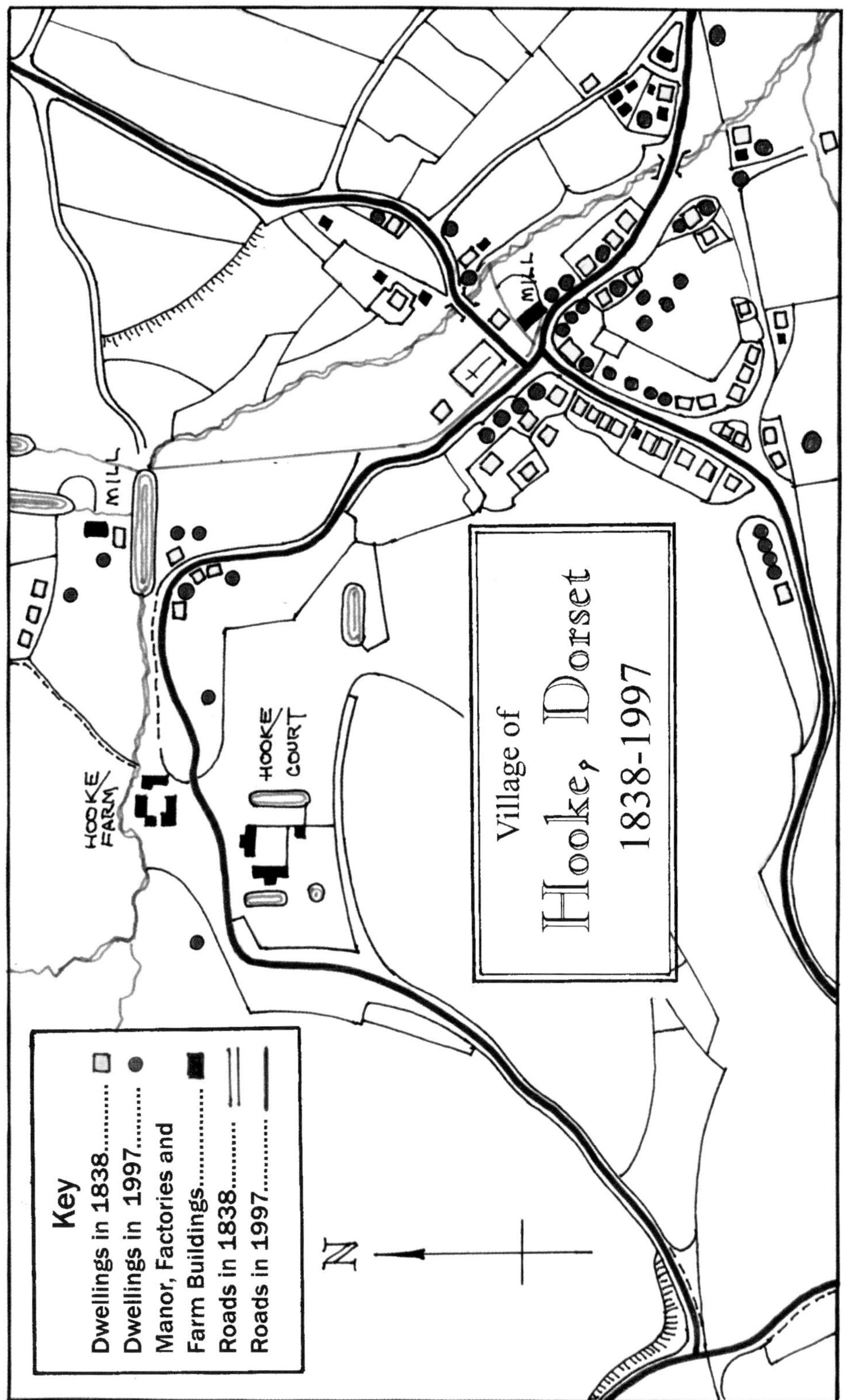

Figure 9.1 **Comparison of Hooke in 1838** (from the Tithe Map) **and 1997**

Old School House was renamed Wellsewn for a time (there is still a stone tablet with that name in the front wall of the house). The owners made curtains, covers and so on and had a shop in Beaminster. The house was set on fire by one of the boys from the school. There were two thatched single storey cottages by the green in 1970 that were demolished to provide space for the two bungalows. The original cottages are probably those mentioned in the RCHM survey of the village.

New houses were built in the 1960s, 1970s and 1990s. The first were the two sets of typical post- war Dorset bungalows in Green Lane and in Kingcombe Road (one of the latter has now been extended to incorporate a first floor). At the other end of the village a small bungalow was built and what looks like a barn conversion opposite. The next development was two houses opposite the church followed by Paulet Close on glebe land. The changes from the time of the tithe map are shown in the diagram on the previous page. The house at Knights-in-the-Bottom had planning permission in 1986 in connection with a fishing business and was ready for occupation in 1990.

Schools at Hooke Court

The following account is drawn mainly from a publication entitled “40 Years On”.

In 1946 the Anglican Franciscans started Saint Francis School for Boys. Brother (later Father) Owen had been in charge of a Remand Home at Cerne Abbas in wartime emergency work. In the opinion of the Brother and his staff there was a big gap in the provision for children “who were unstable and emotionally disturbed, but who were neither mentally nor physically handicapped”. The 1944 Education Act made possible the provision for schools for “maladjusted” children. It was not that easy just to set up a school, finance was a big problem. In order to start a special school, there had to be financial backing before an application could be made to the Ministry of Education. A local farmer provided the £1000 needed as a thanksgiving for regained health and for a successful recent sale. An approach was made to the Ministry for a 50% grant for buildings and equipment, the remaining costs were met by a loan from the generous National Society.

The school was set up in Hooke Court, at that time a somewhat battered, bleak house with a well-worn garden providing a spartan existence. The 17th century wing housed the chapel in the roof space. The stables became workshops and classrooms. Father Owen arrived from the Friary with a few boys in a pony and trap. In 1946 two intrepid females arrived at Hooke by taxi, having come by train to Maiden Newton station. They were accommodated in what is now St. Francis Cottage with iron bedsteads, trunks as tables and candles for light. The school officially opened on Ascension Day in 1946, after much sweeping, scrubbing, polishing. “The army had not long left” - in spite of many requests to residents who lived in Hooke during the war and to various regiments that were near or around Hooke I have been unable to verify that the army was ever there.

In 1947 the farm cottages were converted to make a house for the older boys (Juniper House and the adjoining apartments today). The school’s motto was “Energy and Enthusiasm”, but it took time for the school life to be established, after many unsuccessful experiments, eventually the routine became accepted. Father Owen was a strict disciplinarian, but had a good sense of humour. Most of the boys came from London, Kent and the South West and he would represent the boys who went to court and invariably got them off. Father Owen was the headmaster for the first 20 years, followed by Brother Anselm.

In 1946 the school had a small farm of 150 acres with a farm manager who was assisted by the boys in their free time. The farm had a bull and some cattle. The school farm manager originally lived in a room at Juniper House; later he lived in a bungalow where the large house stands on the hill opposite the lake. The small milking herd and calves had therapeutic value but were a drain on resources. Unfortunately the enterprise was not viable and much of the land was rented out and ultimately sold, although 40 acres were retained. In 1973 most of the stock was sold, sufficient land kept for a rural studies unit with goats, sheep, rabbits and poultry

Some of the boys when they arrived had never slept in a bed; others had never had a bed next to a wall but in the middle of an overcrowded room. Their arrival was a cause for celebration and they put up posters on the walls or drew pictures showing their newfound "luxury"! They were dressed in grey shorts and much of their clothing had to be given to them. There was no central heating only a coke-fired boiler and in some rooms log fires. Brother Simon felled and logged up the trees in the grounds for the fires and for the woodwork shop. The boys helped with the domestic duties (as did the staff) as well as working in the woods and on the farm.

The football field was on Warren Hill, the outline of the field can still be seen from the hedge on the south side of the lane, whereas cricket was played on the field nearer to the school .... on a slope. There were science lessons, there was a pottery, an English room and so on. All the staff went to Mass at 6.30 a.m. every morning, then the boys got up and they all breakfasted together. After breakfast the rooms were tidied and the beds made and the school day commenced.

Christian fellowship, prayer and support were essential features of the school with the Sunday Eucharist as the focal point of the week. Three times each day a bell, hung on the corner between the two wings, was rung. The boys were expected to stand still whilst Father Owen said a short service. The school had its own services in a chapel set up on the top floor of Hooke Court. The basic decorations of that chapel are still there today.

One 10-year old boy was very depressed one winter: he had the 'flu and was in the sick bay. He was not athletic, small for his age, unpopular and often bullied. Brother William unintentionally left his guitar in the room. In the evening, coming to collect his guitar, he was surprised to find that John was picking out tunes on the instrument by ear. John had an exceptional talent and became the lead guitarist in a group called *The Shakedowns,* who became known as the Bridport Beatles. The group played locally, once in Coventry Cathedral and BBC television came and filmed them at school. Some of the former pupils had good careers; some quite high profile including one who went on to play drums with rock legends such as Led Zeppelin and ACDC; he had played with *The Shakedowns*.

A boy called Brian saw a horse advertised "free and would be delivered" in *Horse and Hound*. He took delivery and the horse appeared in many photographs taken at the school, although it eventually died. Brian went on to look after the horses at Sandhurst.

There was an interesting period in 1963 with three months of snow, with the boys ferried from Maiden Newton station in a variety of vehicles through the drifts.

The old East wing of Hooke Court, that was demolished in 1965, had a large kitchen downstairs, a larder, a washing-up room, a corridor facing the moat and, for the boys, a shower room to use after P.E. It was badly damaged by wood beetle (a more likely story than the army leaving it in poor condition). The East wing was demolished, the last remains being burned, almost a repeat of the civil war occurrence. Some of the stones from the North wing (or more usually called the East wing!) were used to build The Little Portion and the rockery in the garden of that house. It was necessary to provide a new building for the school; not the most elegant or sympathetic of designs! The new building caused a lot of excitement with large lorries, a giant crane and much activity from the workmen. The building received a colossal grant from the Ministry of Education, but also from the results of much local fund raising. The new building was luxurious compared with the old spartan existence, but was almost uncomfortable in its newness: carpets in the classrooms; showers and changing rooms in the gym. Today it looks out of place in its setting, but it was felt by those who funded it to be necessary for St. Francis to become a proper school!

In 1979 Jack Barnett, who had previously been deputy, was appointed as headmaster for two years. Father Owen died in 1981.

The school had almost a page to itself in the *Independent* on March 19th 1992 when a financial miracle was needed to keep the school open. A photograph includes the then head, Paul Barry, and Brother Philip along with three pupils and a former pupil. In 1997 the Earl of Sandwich raised the issue in the House of Lords, asking what had happened to the boys who had been cast back on to the streets in the name of savings?

An art teacher, Peter Whiteman, bought the building to use as a foyer scheme for the young homeless, but it was unsuccessful. The current Hooke Court School is a very different school: a private Nursery and Preparatory School. Wessex Educational Trust runs the school and uses the new dormitory buildings for visiting schools on field trips. The main house is used for adult education and for holiday lettings.

The church

The church still had oil lamps after the war, probably like those shown in the photograph in the church taken in 1871. After the Second World War, Wilfred Hepplestone, the gardener at the school, accompanied the services on a violin. He was reputed to walk to Toller Porcorum and also play there. There was a harmonium in the church, but at that time nobody was able to play it (was this, the "organ" that Mrs Parker played?). The South aisle had pews facing north, many with the boys names carved on them. Parson White from Toller was the joint vicar who took the services. The church had heating installed in 1948, presumably using the recently introduced electricity.

The boys from St. Francis School attended a service in the church once a month that was taken by Father Owen. It was a sung mass with a boy swinging incense. The brothers also officiated at other services in St. Giles church.

The East window of the church was designed in 1963 and the faculty for installation was in 1964 in memory of the Parker family (the Reverend T Parker was Rector from 1902 to 1939). The window is the work of Francis W. Skeat. His "signature" changed on windows. He used: 1) a standing hart within a shield; 2) a seated hart with lettering; 3) a standing figure of St. Francis with the artist's initials above his head; 4) outline of St. Alban's Abbey and lettering. Whilst the signature on the East window is the fourth version, it is interesting to note the connections with Hooke for the other signatures: St. Giles' hart and the Franciscans! Francis Skeat moved to Sweden in 1988. In 1965 a memorial tablet was added for the window.

In 1970 the ecclesiastical parish of Hooke was transferred from the rural deanery of Bridport to that of Beaminster. The rights of patronage were transferred in 1974 from Lady Williams to Sir Robert Williams, both of Brideshead. In 1977 seven pews were removed from the South aisle and sold and the floor was made good at that time. The purpose was to provide space for meetings of parishioners. The Parish Meeting occurs in the church two or more times each year. In 1980 a new floor was laid in the South aisle and timbers were replaced in the vestry. The South aisle roof was repaired, new joists put in the nave, and the chancel and tower roofs were repaired.

The village of Hooke made the *Times* again on Tuesday December 23rd, 2003. The Bishop of Salisbury particularly commended "the small parish of Hook in the Beaminster team in his diocese, where there is no organ and worshippers are handed hymn books with the parts for soprano, alto, tenor and bass. The singing is wonderful because they have taken responsibility for it." There may be some exaggerations here; there is an organ that is used, except on the first Sunday of the month when the singing is unaccompanied, and there are no hymn books with parts.

Millennium gate

After much discussion between the Parochial Church Council and the Parish Meeting a Millennium project was decided. John Anderson, who lives in the village, designed the gate to the churchyard from Higher Street Lane (Figure 9.2). A blacksmith in North Dorset made the gate (unfortunately none of the local blacksmiths were interested in doing the work). The gate represents St. Giles through the arrow and the deer and his roles as patron saint of cripples, travellers, and blacksmiths; it also incorporates MM to represent 2000.

Figure 9.2

Design for the millennium gate
by John Anderson
(a resident in the village)

Individuals of Interest

The Goddards

In the first half of the 20th century much of the land was owned by the Goddards including the field opposite the church where there were Church Cottages. Mr Goddard would go out of the village in a pony and trap to a pub and be brought back by the pony. After Mrs Goddard had sold Hooke Court she lived in a caravan on the plot where Hooke Springs Cottage now stands. She had a large white Alsation dog. Mrs Rousell MBE was the cook at the school, her daughter married Mrs Goddard's son Bob.

The cricket pitch was not only used by the village cricket team but also by the boys. The particularly good cricketers are remembered as the Goddards, Mr Pinney and Brother Simon.

The Reverend John Penrose

The Reverend John Penrose was Vicar of the combined parishes of Toller Porcorum and Hooke. He was a bachelor living with his housekeeper in Toller Porcorum, Hooke rectory having been sold as a private house. The churchwarden at Hooke was surprised early one morning to see the church lights on. Investigating she found the bishop, the archdeacon and the vicar of Beaminster officiating at the wedding of John Penrose and his housekeeper. It appears that as he was getting older he became worried about an income for his housekeeper when he died. The bishop suggested that he quietly marry her so that she would get a pension. The wedding was kept secret and even in 2000 a local resident of long standing asked who was the lady marked on the Penrose grave in the north east corner of the churchyard at Hooke?

Mr James Drewitt

Mr Joseph James Drewitt visited the village with his horse-drawn fruit round. He lived in Clift Lane at Toller Porcorum; the pony was called Tommy. He also kept a few cows and chickens and did some thatching of ricks. He moved to the Paulet Arms in 1952, the brewery being Grove Brewery, Weymouth (presumably bought from Devenish during or after the war). The Drewitts kept the pub, and kept pigs; the smell did not please the owners of the Old School House. Publicans had additional businesses as well as being publicans. Perhaps it is not surprising that the pubs have gradually closed in the 20th century when the publicans run no other business. The pub was closed on September 29th 1960 and renamed Paulet Farm, the owners being, amongst other things, agricultural contractors and timber merchants (their headed paper listed: pick up bailing, mowing, cultivating, rotovating, ploughing, spraying, hedge cutting, hay and straw supplied, fencing piles, gate posts, gates, cut timber, contract timber cutting, fire logs!). They also had a small dairy herd, pigs and around 2000 chickens. There were large broiler houses at the back of the house and also on the other side of the river behind The Old School House. A few cows and pigs were kept at Knights-in-the-Bottom. Mrs Drewitt ran the house as a guest house with her sons. Rex, one of the sons, was married in Hooke Church in 1964. The Drewitt grave is in the churchyard at Hooke.

Other people in Hooke

The farm was sold to the Bush family in 1969. They ran it as a guest house and carried out major changes to the garden, raising the level well above the level where the remains may have been for the mill. Reg Bush's son, Barry, used the land next door to build Burnside, removing the sheds and broiler houses.

The dilapidated mill at the Hooke Court end of the village was lived in by Mrs Christian. She was reputed to have used the skirting boards for firewood. When there was a thunderstorm she and her daughters would hide under the stairs. Her daughter Sylvia was killed in a car accident on the way to Beaminster.

Professor and Mrs Margrie lived in Hooke House (the former rectory). She was an artist and produced several drawings of the village that were sold as postcards.

Former residents of the village still have paintings by an amateur artist, Peter Courtney, who was the odd job man at St. Francis School.

Interactions affecting people in the village

Rampisham masts

By 1941 the skyline had changed with the introduction of the Rampisham Radio Masts for the BBC World Service. Some of the people that worked there lived in the village. The masts were replaced and made taller in 1971 to their present layout. The more recent powerful transmitters, now coming to the end of their life, cause much interference to radio and television in the village. There is a special repeater station for television on the mast nearest to the village.

Electricity and water

Electricity came to the valley in about 1947. Water was later, in 1963, and mains drainage has yet to reach Hooke in 2003. "The largest spring I have ever seen used to gush out of the steep hillside, and was immediately used for water cress. Today this is one of the principal sources of supply for the local water board, who have erected a rather expensive but attractive building on site" (Wightman, 1965). In 1963 Hooke's water supply was pumped from a main instead of from ram pumps. The Hooke Pumping Station was one of the two main sources of the West Dorset Water Board when it was opened in 1963. It was a difficult site to work because of the waterlogged state of the peat above greensand. The water was (and still is) tapped from 12 of the springs in the valley below (there is still plenty of water for the Trout Farm). The water from each spring is piped to screening chambers. Through the 36" main there flows 36,000 gallons of water each hour; the water is chlorinated on site. The water was pumped into two reservoirs, a large one on Toller Down and smaller one in Hooke Park (on the left above the bridleway that leads from opposite the road coming from Hooke Court). The one in Hooke Park was filled at night and maintained the pressure during the day. The Toller Down reservoir originally served Beaminster Rural District, Charmouth and Chideock. All the information is sampled through BT lines and dealt with remotely. Only weekly visits to the site are needed unless there is an emergency. The station is now linked to the ring main in Dorset. The water pressure is high in Hooke because of its proximity to the pumping station. The pump house was designed so that its "front elevation is derived from that of the old manor house in the district".

Traffic and public transport

One of the most noticeable changes to the village is the rise in traffic and, particularly, very large tractors, double-decker coaches and articulated low-loader lorries. All these vehicles are widening the lanes. The bus service is subsidised. In the early 1990s it was possible to get to Beaminster and to Bridport one day and back the next. Maiden Newton was feasible in both directions on the same day! By the turn of the century Bridport had become possible in both directions on the same day. The only trouble is that the service is being considered for cutting altogether.

Floods

Floods have continued to plague Hooke. As in Lady Salt's diary in the 1920s (see the last chapter), New Year's Eve seems to be the favourite time for floods. No flood alleviation scheme has been considered. There is some silting of the river by runoff from farmland, particularly from the growing of maize on higher ground. The implications for fish and birds along the river are bleak because the fine silt contains chemicals and also covers the eggs of insects and fish, so damaging the food chain in a devastating way. In addition the excessive use of fertilisers increasing the nitrates in the river has potential implications for drinking water further down stream. The future for the chalk stream looks hopeless unless some action is taken (LEAP, 2000).

Parish Meeting

The parish has continued to have a Parish Meeting rather than elect a parish council, upholding the original 19th century decision. The parish meeting did not meet for a few years in the 1950s as a result of which the village lost the ownership of its village green. The application was made but never confirmed. The Parish meeting now has more planning responsibilities that may provide difficulties amongst neighbours in such a small village. Ultimately it may become increasingly difficult to get volunteers for the key positions of chairman and clerk.

Fund Raising

In spite of a relatively small congregation of about 15, church fund raising continues along traditional lines and is very successful, all the village supporting the retention of the church. Social functions and fund raising events enable the village to have a busy social life without having a village hall. The larger houses and barns are used for many of the functions with others taking place at Toller Porcorum Village Hall.

Population

The 1991 census data included:

Population 113: 63M, 50F;

Householders 36;

Dwellings 35.

Age structure	Percentage	National percentages
0-15	25.66	20.07
16,17	0	2.5
18-44	37.7	39.42
45-Retirement	18.58	19.23
Retirement -	18.58	18.78
85 -	1.77	1.53

Economically Active	49	
Full time Employed	44.9	61.63
Part time Employed	14.24	16.16
Self-employed	40.82	11.76
Unemployed	2.04	9.17
Households	*Percentage*	*National percentages*
Owner occupied	75	67.42
Renting privately	22.22	8.61
Renting publicly	2.78	22.8
Household characteristics		
Lone pensioner	2.86	15.02
Long term illness	14.29	24.60
Lone parents	2.78	4.10
Dependent children	33.33	30.01
Lacking/sharing own bath/shower/WC	5.71	32.41
Without car	5.71	32.41
With 2 or more cars	51.43	23.84
Occupational characteristics		
Professional/Managerial/Technical	50.00	37.54
Skilled Manual/non-manual	0 (surprising)	40.05
Partly skilled, unskilled	0 (surprising)	18.06
Employment Categories		
Agricultural, Forestry. Fishing	0 (obviously an error)	
Manufacturing	0	
Services	75	40.31
With higher qualifications	55.56	13.39

The change in characteristics of the village from 50 years previously is obvious. Clearly it is no longer a dying village. In Appendix E are shown the occupations of the residents in 1995.

Agriculture

Much of the pasture is ploughed and planted with rye grass. Fertilisers and herbicides are applied to provide a wildlife desert with potential long-term damage for future generations. Many of the wild flowers now only exist in the hedgerows and in the woodlands. The hedges are decimated by flailing, removing not only food for the wildlife but also preventing new growth to replenish the hedges. Hedges are too low for birds to nest, too thin to keep livestock in and often need rooting out and re-planting to be of any use.

Watercress farm

In 1967 it was written that "The Hooke river enters the village through a wide expanse of cultivated cress beds. The cress glitters in the sun, sparkling and dazzling to the eye with its glossy leaves. Past the inn the little river babbles away southwards joined by another small spring at Bridge Farm." It was still run by the Goddard family until it was sold in 1973. The estate was sold again in 1973 and the map that was used, was obviously from an earlier date (about 1900!, Figure 9.3).

Dairy farming

After the Second World War dairy farming resumed its predominant place once again. There were three dairy farms in Hooke: Bridge Farm, Manor Farm, Hooke Farm (then called Knap Dairy), being small, these were family run farms. Mechanisation with tractors and machinery, the advent of milk parlours, the potential for storing milk in cooled tanks on site, the extended use of silage, the need for rye grass fields for pasture and for silage have all dramatically changed the countryside around Hooke. One farm has changed to beef cattle and is now organic. Another had financial problems associated with the collapse of Cricket Dairy. The tenant farmer had to reduce from two herds to one and tried growing hemp (under licence!) and flax that was supplied to a company in Cornwall that used the fibres for the linings of car doors. The farmer died as the result of a riding accident and the farm was sold by the owners, The Vesty Trust. A Sussex millionaire farmer now owns most of that farm, running it as a large dairy farm along the lines of New Zealand dairy farms with the cattle being left out in the winter. The other remaining dairy farm is still in the family that was farming in the valley in the late 19th century.

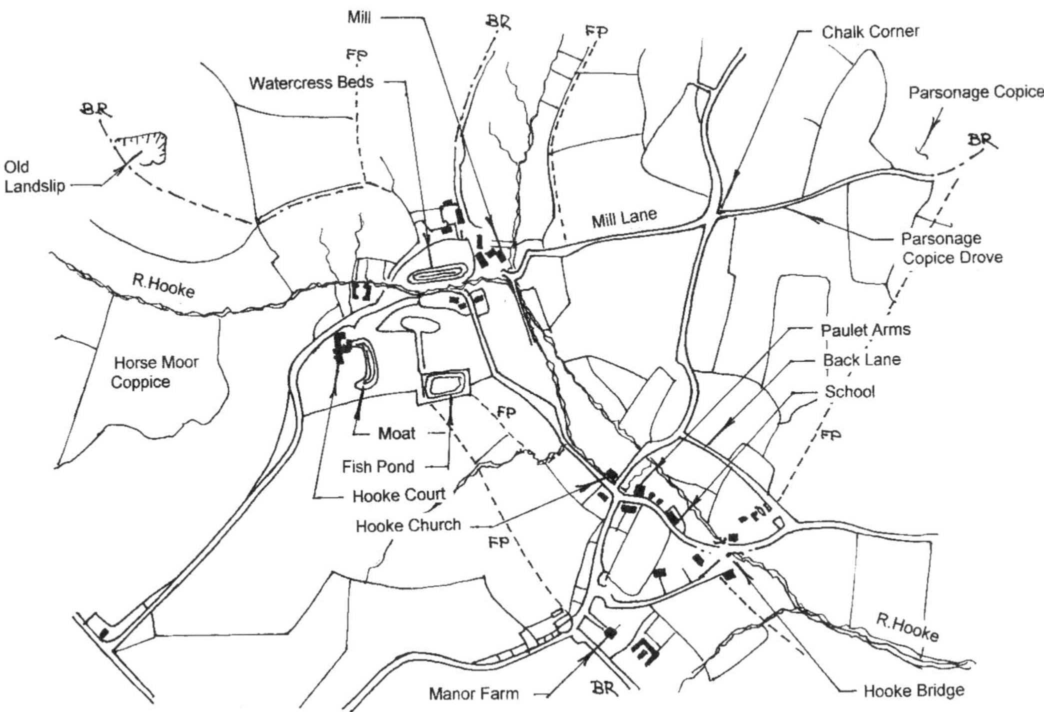

Figure 9.3 **Dated map used for the sale of Hooke Court in 1973** (several features did not exist by then, such as: the Paulet Arms, Parsonage Coppice, School)

Changes in agriculture

After the Second World War, grants were available for the grubbing out of woodlands and coppices to provide arable and pasture. Parsonage Coppice was grubbed out using such a grant. Farming became more intense, requiring more and more fields to be ploughed and replanted with rye grass for the voracious appetites of the Holstein cattle.

As already indicated, maize is grown on higher land for cattle feed. The changes in grants likely to occur as a result of EU decisions will have a dramatic effect on the look of the countryside, but probably will have less effect in Hooke, except perhaps in encouraging less intense farming, thus reducing the amount of livestock. The farmers' incomes are likely to suffer.

The other change is the increase in horses being kept, with associated problems for riders and walkers on the public bridleways and footpaths.

Woodland

Many of the trees were felled and taken to the sawmill at Toller Porcorum during the Second World War. In 1945 there was a start to the devastation of woodland. Hooke Park was sold to the Forestry Commission in 1949 as was an additional 90 acres of rough grazing that now form part of the Park. The wood was planted with beech and conifers, the latter for pit props, so soon not to be needed. The furniture craftsman John Makepeace saw the beech as having potential. Hooke Park was sold to the Parnham Trust in 1983, launched again in 1989 as Hooke Park College, offering students training in the design, product manufacture and enterprise development. The project lasted as long as the government funding was there, but folded in 1994. The trees however did not mature well on the wet ground and have mainly been cut for firewood or for one-off schemes to build using smaller trees. Many more schemes were tried in the park for training young people, but most were financed on short-term grants. Eventually it was proposed to move the Furniture College from Parnham House to the park, but the venture went the way of all the other schemes.

In 2001 Hooke Park became jointly owned by the Architectural Association for use by its undergraduate and postgraduate students in the use of alternative materials for building. It continues as a ground breaking educational programme linked to sustainability, the environment and the craft of construction. Its future looks more secure and it is good to see regular use of the innovative buildings for education (the planning covenant put on them when they were built).

In 2002 it was proposed to manage the woods by felling all the beech and conifer to be replaced with ash because they are self-seeding! Such is progress. However, on a very wet area in the wood, some very old alder trees remain that hopefully will be left.

Westcombe Coppice has had little management for perhaps 80 years and the trees are beginning to fall down. It is unsuitable for government grants because it has no easy access from a road.

Both of these woods are renowned for their displays of bluebells.

Wild boar

In 1997 escaped boar from a farm at Mapperton became wild and were breeding fast. They were "ploughing" fields and becoming a nuisance. A concerted culling regime has controlled the numbers since that time.

Farmers' Radio Station

In order to try to encourage farmers, and to help with the isolation of farmers and their families, a radio station was set up on Dorset by Trilith and started to function in 2004. It trained women to become reporters, one of whom was Helen Wallbridge of Hooke. Her first feature was about the Fooks family of North Poorton (her own family).

Hooke survives

Since 1947 Hooke has changed from a village belonging to a banking family owner, through a rapidly diminishing population focused on St. Francis School and the "naughty boys," to a population of active or recently retired business and professional people.

Farming and its attributes were the historical mainstay of the village; today there are three farmers and two smallholders. By the late 1970s there was only one child under 18 whereas in 2003 there were over 30, showing also a rapid reduction in the average age of the population.

After 550 years of dependency on the neglect, whims, fancies and sometimes the paternalism of knights, marquis's, earls and dukes the village has had just over 50 years determining its own future; quite a responsibility. A village plan could be crucial.

Sources

Chapter 1

Beard E (1995) **Geology and Scenery of Dorset** Bradford-on-Avon, Ex Libris Press

Edwards B (1994) **The Archaeology and Development of the Village of Hooke, West Dorset** (Dissertation from Bournemouth University; a copy is held in Beaminster Museum)

Fagerston A (1933) **The Place Names of Dorset** Uppsala, A-B Lundequistska Bokhandeln (reprinted in 1978 by E. P. Publications Ltd., Wakefield)

Hutchings M (1967) **Hardy's River** Sherborne, The Abbey Press

Rackham O (2001) **The History of the Countryside** London, Phoenix Press

Taylor C (2004) **The Making of the English Landscape Dorset** Wimborne. The Dovecote Press

Winchester S (2001) **The Map that changed the World** London, Penguin Books

White J ((2003) **Downs, Meadows and Pastures** (Discover Dorset series), Wimborne, The Dovecote Press

Wilson V, Welch F B A, Robbie J A, Green G W (1958) **The Geology of the Country around Bridport and Yeovil** London, HMSO

Chapter 2

Aston M and Lewis C (Ed) (1994) **The Medieval Landscape of Wessex** Oxford, Oxbow Books

Edwards B (1994) **The Archaeology and Development of the Village of Hooke, West Dorset** (Dissertation from Bournemouth University; a copy is held in Beaminster Museum)

Eyton R W (1878) **A Key to Domesday** (showing the method and exactitude of its mensurals, and the precise meaning of its more usual formulae: Analysis and Digest of the Dorset Survey.) London, Taylor and Co.

Fagerston A (1933) **The Place Names of Dorset** Uppsala, A-B Lundequistska Bokhandeln (reprinted in 1978 by E. P. Publications Ltd., Wakefieldl)

Field N H (1992) **Dorset and the Second Legion. New Light on a Roman Campaign.** Tiverton, Dorset Books

Hutchins J (1863) **The History and Antiquities of The County of Dorset Vol. 2** Westminster, John Bowyer Nichols and Sons.

Landels J G (1997) **Engineering in the Ancient World** London, Constable (originally published in 1978 by Chatto and Windus)

Leach P (2001) **Roman Somerset** Wimborne, The Dovecote Press

Page W (Ed) **Victoria History of Dorset Volume II** Oxford University Press

Page W (Ed) **Victoria History of Dorset Volume III** Oxford, Oxford University Press

Pugh R B (Ed) (1968) **The Victorian History of the Counties of England** London, The University of London Institute of Historical Research

Rackham O (2001) **The History of the Countryside** London, Phoenix Press

Salway P (1981) **Roman Britain** Oxford History of Britain, Oxford, Oxford University Press

Stenton, Sir F (1971) **Anglo-Saxon England** Oxford History of Britain, Oxford, Oxford University Press

Taylor C (2004) **The making of the English Landscape Dorset** Wimborne. The Dovecote press

The Church of St. Giles and the Village of Hooke Dorset, (Undated)

Timperley H W, Brill E (1965) **Ancient Trackways of Wessex** London, Phoenix House pp 50,51.

Chapter 3

Bettey J H (1974) **Dorset** Newton Abbott, David and Charles (City and County Histories) pg. 76

Backhouse J (1999) **The Sherborne Missal** London, The British Library

Cal Inquisitions post Mortem Vol. 2 (Edward j) p 231
Source: card index Dorset County Museum

Cantor L M, Wilson J D (1962) The Mediaeval Deer Parks of Dorset 1 **Proc of Dorset Nat Hist and Arch Soc 83, 114-116**

de Banco Roll No 212A Michaelmas, 9 Edward ij, Fry's **TSS** Vol. H 2 Pg. 395
M 186 Dorset
Source: card index Dorset County Museum

de Banco Roll No 213 Hilary 9 Edward ij Fry's **TSS** M 248d Dorset
Source: card index Dorset County Museum

de Banco Roll No 219 Easter 8 Edward ij Fry's **TSS** Vol. H 1 Pg. 370
M 212 Dorset

Source: card index Dorset County Museum

"Deer parks in Dorset and Somerset" **Somerset and Dorset Notes and Queries, V,** 83-87

Edwards B (1994) **The Archaeology and Development of the Village of Hooke, West Dorset** (Dissertation from Bournemouth University; a copy is held in Beaminster Museum)

Eyton R W (1878) **A Key to Domesday** showing the method and exactitude of its mensurals, and the precise meaning of its more usual formulae: Analysis and Digest of the Dorset Survey. London, Taylor and Co.

Fagerston A (1933) **The Place Names of Dorset** Uppsala, A-B Lundequistska Bokhandeln

(reprinted in 1978 by E. P. Publications Ltd., Wakefield)

Feat of Fines Fry's **Dorset Records** Vol. 10 Pg. 13
Source: card index Dorset County Library

Field N H (1992) **Dorset and the Second Legion. New Light on a Roman Campaign.** Tiverton, Dorset Books

Fry E A and Fry GS (1910) **Dorset Records: Dorset Feet of Fines 1327-1485** (in County Museum Library)

Good R (1979, 1987 edition) **The Lost Villages of Dorset** Wimborne, The Dovecote Press

Handwritten History of Hooke, Dorset County Record Office Record no. E175A

Hibbert C (1994) **The English: A Social History 1066-1945** London, Harper Collins

Hutchins J (1863) **The History and Antiquities of The County of Dorset Vol. 2** Westminster, John Bowyer Nichols and Sons.

Miller A (1999) **The Monastaries of Dorset ,** Albermarle Books (Pg 182)

Mills A D (Ed) (1971) **The Dorset Lay Subsidy Roll of 1332** Dorchester, Dorset Records Society

Mills A D (1986) **Dorset place Names, Their Origins and Meanings** Wimborne, Roy Casson Books

Page W (Ed) **Victoria History of Dorset Volume II** Oxford University Press

Page W (Ed) **Victoria History of Dorset Volume III** Oxford, Oxford University Press

PRO Subsidy Roll No 103/5 Copy on Pope's mss in Dorset County Museum, Pg. 64
Source: card index in Dorset County Museum

PRO Calendar Patent Rolls 18 Edward III Jan 1344 from Brebner P (1997) **Hooke Court, Beaminster, Dorset: Outline of Historical Development** (Only copy held by Mr Peter and Mrs Mandy Cooper)

Rackham O (2001) **The History of the Countryside** London, Phoenix Press

RCHM (1939) Record Card of Earthworks giving details of Hooke Court and the church.

Rotuli Hundredum, I, 98
Source: card index Dorset County Museum

Rumble A R (1980) **The Dorset Lay Subsidy Roll of 1327 D**orchester, Dorset Record Society Publication No.6

Taylor C (2004) **The making of the English Landscape Dorset** Wimborne. The Dovecote Press

The Book of Fees (Testa de Nevill) Vol. 1 Pg. 424
Source: card index Dorset County Museum

The Church of St. Giles and the Village of Hooke Dorset (Undated)

Timperley H W, Brill E (1965) **Ancient Trackways of Wessex** London, Phoenix House pp 50,51.

Uglow J (2004) **A Little History of British Gardening** London, Chatto and Windus

Chapter 4

Bennett W (1987) **The Toller Whelme Book** Toller Whelme, Dorset (Printed by Creeds Printers)

Bettey J H (1974) **Dorset** Newton Abbott, David and Charles

Bettey J H (2003) "Alehouse Gossip and Church Reform in Somerset 1539" **Notes and Queries for Somerset and Dorset, 35,** Part 358, 236-239

Cantor L M, Wilson J D (1962) The Mediaeval Deer Parks of Dorset 1 **Proc of Dorset Nat History and Archaeological Society 83,** 114-116

Cuming G J (1982) **A History of Anglican Liturgy** London, Macmillan Press

Dictionary of National Biography Vol XVIII , 861-862

Duffy Eamon (1992) **The Stripping of the Altars** New Haven USA, Yale University Press

Duffy Eamon (2001) **The Voices of Morebath, Reformation and Rebellion in an English Village** New Haven, USA. Yale University Press.

Edwards B (1994) **The Archaeology and Development of the Village of Hooke, West Dorset** (Dissertation from Bournemouth University; a copy is held in Beaminster Museum)

Fry E A and Fry GS (1910) **Dorset Records: Dorset Feet of Fines 1327-1485** (in County Museum Library)

Feudal Aids Vol. II Pg. 105)
Source: card index Dorset County Museum

Gibbs J. H. P. (undated, about 1980) **Fan Vaults and Medieval Sculpture of Sherborne Abbey** Sherborne, The Friends of Sherborne Abbey.

Good R (1966) **The Old Roads of Dorset** (Enlarged Edition), Bournemouth, Horace G Cummins Ltd.

Hearing T (1999) **Dorset Justice** Poole, The Magistrates Association – Dorset Branch

Hibbert C (1994) **The English: A Social History 1066-1945** London, Harper Collins

Handwritten History of Hooke Dorset County Record Office Record no. E175A

Newman J, Pevsner N (1972) **The Buildings of England: Dorset** Harmondsworth, Penguin

Medieval Items **Proceedings of the Dorset Natural History and Archaeological Society, 23,** 1-3.

Page W (Ed) **Victoria History of Dorset Volume III** Oxford, Oxford University Press

Penrose J (1964) **Historic Hook and its Nationally Acclaimed Church** (It would appear that this was a leaflet produced for sale in the church. Revd Penrose was the vicar of Toller Porcorum and Hooke combined parish. The choice of spelling of Hooke is interesting.)

PRO Subsidy Rolls Box 103- Nos. 70, 71 [**Feudal Aids, Dorset Vol. II** Pg. 76]) Source: card index Dorset County Museum

RCHM (1952) **An Inventory of the Historical Monuments of Dorset Vol 1 West**

Taylor C (2004) **The making of the English Landscape Dorset** Wimborne. The Dovecote press

The Church of St. Giles and the Village of Hooke Dorset (Undated)

Chapter 5

Bennett W (1987) **The Toller Whelme Book** (printed by Creeds the Printers)

Betty J. H. (1996) **Man and the Land. 150 Years of Dorset Farming 1846-1996** Dorchester, Dorset Natural History & Archaeological Society

Brebner P (1997) **Hooke Court, Beaminster, Dorset. Outline of Historical Development** (private document sent to Mandy and Peter Cooper who let me see a copy)

Cantor L M, Wilson J D (1962) The Mediaeval Deer Parks of Dorset 1 **Proc of Dorset Nat Hist and Arch Soc 83, 114-116**

"Church Bells" **Proceedings of Dorset Natural History and Archaeological Society, 25,** 45

Civil Division of the County of Dorset 1833 (2nd Edition) Dorchester

Dacombe M R (Ed) (1936) **Dorset up Along and Down Along** (A collection of History, Tradition, Folk Lore, Flower Names and Herbal Lore) (gathered together by Women's institutes) (2nd edition) Dorchester, Longmans

Edwards B (1994) **The Archaeology and Development of the Village of Hooke, West Dorset** (Dissertation from Bournemouth University; a copy is held in Beaminster Museum)

Eedle M de G (1984) **A History of Beaminster** Chichester, Phillimore and Co. Ltd. Pg. 34

Evans H (1913) **Our Old Nobility** London, Daily News and Reader

Gerard T (1625, but attributed to Coker 1732) **Survey of Dorset**

Good R (1940) **The Old Roads of Dorset** Dorchester, Longmans.

Goodwin T (1996) **Dorset in the Civil War (1625-1665)** Tiverton, Dorset Books

Handwritten History of Hooke, Dorset County Record Office Record no. E175A

Hearing T (1999) **Dorset Justice** Poole, The Magistrates Association – Dorset Branch

Hibbert C (1994) **The English: A Social History 1066-1945** London, Harper Collins

Hindle S (University of Warwick 1997) P**ower, Welfare Policy and Social Relationships in England 1600 –1834** DNHAAS Day School on Pov*erty and the Poor Law in the Nineteenth Century*

Hine R (1914) **History of Beaminster,** Taunton, Barnicott and Pearce

Hunt & Co (1851) **Directory of Dorsetshire** London, (printed) BW Gardiner

Hutchins J (1863) **The History and Antiquities of The County of Dorset Vol. 2** Westminster, John Bowyer Nichols and Sons,

Page W (Ed) **Victoria History of Dorset Volume III** Oxford, Oxford University Press

Lloyd R (1967) **Dorset Elizabethans** London, John Murray

Nichloson A (2003) **Power and Glory: Jacobean England and the making of the King James Bible** London, Harper Collins

Newman J, Pevsner N (1972) **The Buildings of England: Dorset** Harmondsworth, Penguin

Nightingale J E (1889) **Diocese of Salisbury. The Church Plate of Dorset** Bennett Bros. Dorset

O'Shea M (2000) Letters about the Mintern(e) family.

Rackham O (2001) **The History of the Countryside** London, Phoenix Press

RCHM (1952) **An Inventory of the Historical Monuments of Dorset Vol 1 West**

Reid R (1989) **The Georgian House and its details** London, Bishopsgate Press Ltd.

RCHM (1952) **An Inventory of the Historical Monuments of Dorset Vol 1 West**

(1917) "A Political Sermon at Hooke in 1626" **Somerset and Dorset Notes and Queries Vol.XV**

Stanier P (1998) **The Industrial Past** Discover Dorset Series, Wimborne, Dovecote Press.

Taylor C (2004) **The Making of the English Landscape Dorset** Wimborne. The Dovecote press

The Church of St. Giles and the Village of Hooke Dorset (Undated)

Woodforde J (1969) **The Truth about Cottages** London, Routledge and Kegan Paul

Chapter 6

Bennett W (1987) **The Toller Whelme Book** (printed by Creeds the Printers)

Bettey J H (1974) **Dorset** Newton Abbott, David and Charles

Bolton Estate records for a large number of documents relating to Hooke including Manorial Court records, Hooke Estate papers (all held at the Dorset Record Office: examples used: Court Books D/MAP M1-17; estate papers E101,111,175,175A)

Boswell E (1833) **Civil Division of the County of Dorset 1795** (2nd Edition) Dorchester, Weston, Simonds and Sydenham

Brocklebank J (1979) **Victorian Stone Carvers in Dorset Churches** Wimborne, The Dovecote Press.

Dacombe M R (Ed) (1951) D**orset: Up Along Down Along** (3rd Edition) Dorchester, Longmans Ltd.

Dorset Farming from 16th century to the 17th century University of Bristol Continuing Education Course at The County Museum, Dorchester, 1995.

Edwards B (1992) Excavation **Proceedings of Dorset Natural History and Archaelogy Society, 114,** 234

Edwards B (1994) **The Archaeology and Development of the Village of Hooke, West Dorset** (Dissertation from Bournemouth University; a copy is held in Beaminster Museum)

Good R (1940) **The Old Roads of Dorset** Dorchester, Longmans.

Hayward G (2003) "The Hayward: a Manorial Official" **Somerset and Dorset Queries XXXV,** 249 -253

Hibbert C (1994) **The English: A Social History 1066-1945** London, Harper Collins

Page W (Ed) **Victoria History of Dorset Volume III** Oxford, Oxford University Press

Penrose J (1964) **Historic Hook and its Nationally Acclaimed Church** (It would appear that this was a leaflet produced for sale in the church. Revd Penrose was the vicar of Toller Porcorum and Hooke combined parish.)

Rackham O (2001) **The History of the Countryside** London, Phoenix Press

Sadler M and P (Undated) **Corscombe through the Ages** (printed by Creeds the Printers)

Stanier P. H. (1993) Dorset limekilns: a first survey **Proceedings of Dorset Natural History and Archaeological Society, 115,** 33-49

Tomalin C (2002) **Samuel Pepys: the Unequalled Self** London, Viking

Taylor C (2004) **The Making of the English Landscape Dorset** Wimborne. The Dovecote press

Chapter 7

Addleshaw G W O and Etchells F (1948) **The Architectural Setting of Anglican Worship** London, Faber and Faber Limited

Beatty C J P (1991) **Thomas Hardy and the Restoration of Rampisham Church** (Printed by Creeds the Printers, Broadoak, Bripdort)

Bennett W (1987) **The Toller Whelme Book** (printed by Creeds the Printers)

Bettey J H (1974) **Dorset** Newton Abbott, David and Charles

Bettey J.H. (1996) **Man and the Land: Farming in Dorset 1946-1996** Dorchester, DNHAAS

Bolton Estate records for a large number of documents relating to Hooke including Manorial Court records, Hooke Estate papers (all held at the Dorset Record Office: examples used: Court Books D/MAPM1-17; estate papers E101,111,175,175A)

Bridport News Various extracts from "100 Years Ago".

Crowther M A "The Workhouse" in Smart T C (Ed) (1992) **Victorian Values** London, The British Academy

"Church Restoration" **Proceedings of Dorset Natural History and Archaeological Society, 39,** 101

Civil Division of the County of Dorset 1833 (2nd Edition) Dorchester

Dorsetshire and Somersetshire Chronicle 16th May 1895 "Toller Whelme"

Dorset County Council (1978) **Dorset countryside treasures in W Dorset District Part 1** Dorchester, Dorset Countryside Treasures Pg 74

Dorset County Council (1979) **Dorset countryside treasures**: **Dorset Workhouses** Dorchester, Dorset Countryside Treasures.

Dorset County Council (1980) **Dorset countryside treasures in W Dorset District Part 2** Dorchester, Dorset Countryside Treasures Pg 72

Dorset Farming from 16th century to the 17th century University of Bristol Continuing Education Course at The County Museum, Dorchester, 1995.

Eedle M de G (1984) **A History of Beaminster** Chichester, Phillimore and Co. Ltd. (Pg. 138)

Edwards B (1993) Excavations **Proceedings of Dorset Natural History and Archaeological Society, 115,** 151

Edwards B (1994) **The Archaeology and Development of the Village of Hooke, West Dorset** (Dissertation from Bournemouth University; a copy is held in Beaminster Museum)

Enumeration Abstract (1881) Volume 1

Flame M (1997) **The Dorset Gentry and Poor Law Reform** DNHAAS Day School on Pov*erty and the Poor Law in the Nineteenth Century* (author from De Montfort University, Leicester,

Fowler J (1951) **Medieval Sherborne** Dorchester, Longmans

Hibbert C (1994) **The English: A Social History 1066-1945** London, Harper Collins

Hooke Parish Meeting Minute Booke (1894-1950) Copy held at Dorset Record Office

Hooke PCC Minutes Most held by the PCC in a safe in the church (apply to the church wardens)

Hutchings M (1967) **Hardy's River** Sherborne, The Abbey Press

James J (1998) **The Victorians** Discovering Dorset, Wimborne, The Dovecote Press

Kelly E. R. (1885) **County Topographics: Dorsetshire** London, Kelly G

Kelly's (1915) **Kelly's Directory**

Kay-Robinson D (1984) **The Landscape of Thomas Hardy** Exeter, Webb and Bower

Lists of Indoor and Outdoor poor chargeable to the parish of Beaminster with statements of account of the Beaminster Union 1849-53, 1857-8 copy held at Dorset Record Office,Dorchester

Mabey W (1930) **The history and Life of William Mabey written from Memory at 82 years of age** copy held at Dorset Record Office,Dorchester.

Mansfield P (2003) "The Somerset Peasantry" **Notes and Queries from Somerset and Dorset, 35**, part 358, 258-167.

Page W (Ed) **Victoria History of Dorset Volume III** Oxford, Oxford University Press

Rackham O (2001) **The History of the Countryside** London, Phoenix Press

Sherry D (1970) **Dorset Trades and Crafts** Swanage, The Purbeck Press

Stanier P (1998) **The Industrial Past** Discover Dorset Series, Wimborne, Dovecote Press.

Taylor C (2004) **The Making of the English Landscape Dorset** Wimborne. The Dovecote Press

Trades Union Congress (1934) **The Book of the Martyrs of Tolpuddle 1834-1934** London, The Trades Union Congress General Council

Westonzoyland Engine Trust (1996) **The Hydraulic Ram** (Information Booklet No. 4)

Winchester S (2001) **The Map that changed the World** London, Penguin Books

Chapter 8

"Visit by Mr Hillman October 2002". A walk through Hooke with Mr Hillman: notes of the conversation that took place.

Bettey J.H. (1996) **Man and the Land: Farming in Dorset 1946-1996** Dorchester, DNHAAS

Bush R (undated) handwritten extract from (?)Kelly's Directory 1841.

Drewitt, C (1999, 200) Letters to the author

Fowler J (1951) **Medieval Sherborne** Dorchester, Longmans

Dorset Countryside Treasures (1979) **Dorset Workhouses** Dorchester, Dorset Countryside Treasures.

Edwards B (1994) **The Archaeology and Development of the Village of Hooke, West Dorset** (Dissertation from Bournemouth University; a copy is held in Beaminster Museum)

Gibb J H P (about 1980) **Fan Vaults and Medieval Sculpture of Sherborne Abbey** Sherborne, Friends of Sherborne Abbey.

Harris D (2003) **Officers. South Africa. 1900-1901. 1902** (A copy made from a bound photograph album with hand-written details of the 47 officers.) Copies are held at: Beaminster

Museum; Hooke Court; Military Museum, Chelsea.

Hearing T (1999) **Dorset Justice** Poole, The Magistrates Association – Dorset Branch

Hibbert C (1994) **The English: A Social History 1066-1945** London, Harper Collins

Hine J (1986) "The First World War Beaminster 1914 – 1919" in **Ancient but Modern – Recollections from the Countryside Selected for Beaminster Area Team News** (Ed. T Biles)

Hooke Parish Meeting Minutes (the minutes from 1894 to about 1950 are held in the Dorset Record office. There is a gap of several years. More recent records are held by the parish clerk.

Hooke PCC Minutes (These are mainly stored in the church and the churchwardens need to be contacted for access.)

Mitchell V, Smith K (1994) **Yeovil to Dorchester including Branch Line to Bridport** Midhurst, W Sussex, Middleton Press

Newman J, Pevsner N (1972) **The Buildings of England: Dorset** Harmondsworth, Penmuin

Page W (Ed) **Victoria History of Dorset Volume III** Oxford, Oxford University Press

Rackham O (2001) **The History of the Countryside** London, Phoenix Press

Stanier P (1998) **The Industrial Past** Discover Dorset Series, Wimborne, Dovecote Press.

"The Hooke Source and Pumping Station" **The Harland Magazine** Summer 1967

Salt E M, Lady (1920-1930) *Personal Diaries* **(**Extracts provided by her family)

Webster B (2001) Letter to the author

Chapter 9

"A walk through Hooke with Babs Draper" (26/06/2003) notes of the conversation that took place.

Addison J (1968) "Dorset Watermills: Second Addendum" **Transactions of the Newcomen Society XCLI,** 139-162

Bettey J.H. (1996) **Man and the Land: Farming in Dorset 1946-1996** Dorchester, DNHAAS

Burden R and Le Pard G (1996) **A New View of Dorset** Tiverton, Dorset Books

Drewitt C (1999, 2000) Letters about village history.

Edwards B (1994) **The Archaeology and Development of the Village of Hooke, West Dorset** (Dissertation from Bournemouth University; a copy is held in Beaminster Museum)

Hooke Parish Meeting Minutes (the minutes from 1894 to about 1950 are held in the Dorset Record office. There is a gap of several years. The parish clerk holds more recent records.)

Hooke PCC Minutes (These are mainly stored in the church and the churchwardens need to be contacted for access.)

LEAP (2000) **Frome, Piddle and Poole Harbour and Purbeck Local Environment Agency Plan** Blandford Forum, Environment Agency

St Francis School, Hooke Beaminster (1986) **40 Years On: Memories through the years 1946-1986** Hooke, St. Francis School

Taylor C (2004) **The making of the English Landscape Dorset** Wimborne. The Dovecote Press

The Hooke Source and Pumping Station (1967), **The Harland Magazine,** Summer 1967

Webster B (1999) Letter with details of Francis Skeat

Wightman, R (1965) **Portrait of Dorset** London, Robert Hel

Appendix A

Manorial Court

(Owners, Stewards, Tithingmen, and attendances at Court)

Owner

1708 Charles, Duke of Bolton
1753 Lavinia, Duchess Dowager of Bolton
1760 Charles, Duke of Bolton
1765 Harry, Duke of Bolton
1795 Katherine, Duchess of Bolton
1821 Right Honourable Mary Ann Julia Louisa Countess Dowager of Sandwich and the Right Honourable Henry Vane, Duke of Cleveland

Stewards (showing first year of appointment)

1708 Thomas Coward
1715 Jacob Cross
1732 James Cross
1742 Francis Loggin
1744 Morgan Keene
1753 Henry Edwards (deputy)
1755 Henry Edwards *(now steward?)*
1760 Francis Parry
1761 George Durnford
1771 Thomas Lane
1790 Arthur Farwell
1808 George Farwell (deputy)
1809 George Farwell
1811-1820 no records
1821 George Farwell *(last named steward in 1839; no steward named from 1840)*

Bailliff (showing first year of appointment)

1708 Samuel Stevens
1713 Samuel Shepherd
1719 Samuel Stephens
1729 George Stephens
1740 James Daniell
1748 Thomas Crode
No Bailliff mentioned after 1783

Tithingman

1708 William Hopkins
1709 John Williams
1710 Abraham Everett
1711 (no name, Abraham continues?)
1712 (no name, Abraham continues?)
1713 John Williams
1714 (no name, John continues?)
1715 (no name, John continues?)
1716 Thomas Williams
1717 (Sarah Williams to provide tithingman)
1718 (Henry Minterne to provide tithingman)
1719 John Williams, the miller
1720 John Legg
1721 Abraham Everett
1722 Thomas Williams
1723 (Sarah Williams the Younger to provide tithingman)
1724 John Williams
1725 John Legg
1726 John Williams
1727 Charles Williams
1728 Thomas Williams
1729 (no name, Thomas continues?)
1730 (no name, Thomas continues?)
1731 (no name, Thomas continues?)

Haywards

1732 Edward Randall
1733 (no name, Edward continues?)
1734 Edward Randall
1735 Edward Randall
1736 (no name, Edward continues?)
1737 (no name, Edward continues?)
1738 (no name, Edward continues?)
1739 (no name, Edward continues?)
1740 (no name, Edward continues?)
1741 Samuel Legg
1742 Samuel Legg
1743 Samuel Legg
1744 Samuel Legg
1745 Samuel Legg
1746 Samuel Legg
1747 (no name, Samuel continues?)
1748 Samuel Legg
1749 Thomas Short
1750 (no name, Thomas continues?)
1751 Edward Randall
1752 Edward Randall
1753 Edward Randall
1754 Edward Randall
1755 Robert Coombes
1756 Edward Randall
1757 Edward Randall
1758 Edward Randall
1759 Edward Randall
1760 Edward Randall
1761 Edward Randall
1762 Edward Randall
1763 Edward Randall
1764 Edward Randall
1765 Ann Randall
1766 John Short
1767 (no name, John continues?)
1768 John Short
1769 Edward Randall
1770 John Short
1771 John Short
1772 John Short
1773 John Short
1774 John Short
1775 John Short
1777 John Short
1778 John Short
1779 John Short
1780 John Short
1781 John Short
1782 John Short
1783 John Short
1784 John Short
1785 John Short
1786 Henry Minterne
1787 Henry Minterne
1788 Henry Minterne
1789 Henry Cornick
1790 Henry Cornick
1791 Henry Minterne
1792 Henry Minterne
1793 Henry Minterne
1794 (no name, Henry continues?)
1795 Henry Minterne
1796 Henry Minterne
1797 Henry Minterne
1798 Henry Minterne
1799 Henry Minterne
1800 Henry Minterne
1801 Henry Minterne
1802 Robert Hansford
1803 John Pope1804
William Bartlett1805
William Bartlett1806
William Bartlett1807
William Bartlett1808
William Bartlett1809
William Bartlett1810
William Spencer
1811-1820 *records are missing* (Historical Manuscript Commission)
1821 Richard Forsey
1822 Richard Forsey
1823 Richard Forsey
1824 (no name Richard continues?)
1825 Daniel Forsey
1826 Daniel Forsey
1827 William Shiner
1828 (no name, William continues?)
1829 Eubin Cornick
1830 Daniel Forsey
1831 Samuel Mintern
1832 Samuel Mintern
1833 Samuel Mintern
1834 Samuel Mintern
1835 Samuel Mintern
1836 Richard Forsey
1837 Daniel Forsey
1838 (no name, Daniel continues?)
1839 Daniel Forsey
1840 William Walbridge
1841 William Forsey
1842 William Forsey
1843 William Forsey
1844 William Forsey
1845 David Legg
1846 David Legg
1847 David Legg
1848 David Legg
1849 David Legg
1850 David Legg
1851 William Forsey

Manorial Court

(Anyone wishing to investigate earlier records from 1661, these are held at the Hampshire Record Office; the following details are from the records held at the Dorset Record Office.)

1708, 1709	Samuel Minterne, John Williams, William Webber, Benjamin Williams, George Webber, Angell Short, Edward Porter
1710	Samuel Minterne, John Legg, William Webber, Thomas Harding, Samuel Webber, Abraham Everett
1711	(no names)
1712	(no names)
1713	William Webber, john Williams, Angell Short, Thomas Wood, Samuel Webber, George Webber, John Jacob, Edmund Porter
1714	Abraham Everett, William Webber, Angell Short, John Wood, Benjamin Wood, George Webber, John Legg, John Jacob, Samuel Webber, Thomas Harding
1715	Abraham Everett, William Wood (alias Baker), Angell Short, John Wood, Thomas Wood, William Webber, John Legg, Edmund Porter, John Jacob.
1716	Abraham Everett, Angell Short, John Williams, Samuel Minterne, John Moolam.
1717	Abraham Everett, Angell Short, John Williams, William Webber, John Moolam.
1718	Abraham Everett, Angell Short, John Williams, William Webber, John Moolam, David Porter, Samuel Webber, David Williams, John Legg,
1719	Abraham Everett, John Williams, William Webber, Samuel Webber, John Legg, Thomas Harding, Benedictus Pound, William Jacob, John Pound
1720	Abraham Everett, John Williams, William Webber, Benjamin Williams
1721	Abraham Everett, John Williams, William Webber, John Legg, Angell Short, John Woollam
1722	no names
1723	Abraham Everett, John Williams, Angell Short, Edmund Porter
1724	Abraham Everett, William Webber, William Porter, John Legg
1725	Samuel Minterne, Angell Short, John Legg, John Williams, Edmund Porter, William Jacob,
1726	Samuel Minterne, Angell Short, John Williams, Edmund Porter, William Jacob,
1727	Samuel Minterne, Angell Short, John Williams, Thomas Williams, William Webber,
1728	Samuel Minterne, Angell Short, John Williams, Thomas Williams, William Webber, Edmund Porter, William Jacob,
1730	Samuel Minterne, Abraham Everett, Thomas Williams, Matthew Webber
1731	Samuel Minterne, William Webber,
1732	Samuel Minterne, Abrus (Abraham?) Everett, William Webber,
1733	Edward Porter, Angell Short, William Webber, John Crane, William Crane, Henry Cornick
1734	Samuel Minterne, Angell Short, William Webber, Edward Porter, William Crane
1735	Edward Porter, William Crane, Henry Cornick
1736	Edward Porter, Angell Short, William Webber, George Crane
1737	Edward Porter, William Jacob, William Crane, George Crane
1738	William Crane, George Crane
1740	Samuel Minterne, Joseph Legg, Edward Porter, George Crane, John Webber
1741	Samuel Minterne, William Porter, John Moolam, William Crane, George Crane
1742	Samuel Minterne, George Crane, Henry Cornick
1743	Samuel Minterne, John Moolam, William Crane,
1744	John Moolam, Samuel Minterne, John Webber, William Crane, George Crane
1745	Samuel Minterne, Samuel Minterne (jnr), George Crane, William Crane,
1746	Samuel Minterne, John Moolam, Samuel Minterne (jnr), George Crane, William Crane,
1747	John Moolam, William Crane, George Crane
1748	John Moolam, Isaac Everett, John Webber, William Crane, Henry Cornick
1749	Samuel Everett, Joseph Legg, William Crane, Thomas Strode
1750	Isaac Everett, Joseph Legg, William Crane, Thomas Strode
1751	Isaac Everett, Humphry Williams, Samuel Brown, Thomas Strode
1752	Isaac Everett, Humphry Williams, Thomas Strode, William Crane, Samuel Brown,
1753	Isaac Everett, Humphrey Williams, Thomas Strode, William Crane, Samuel Brown, John Webber,
1754	Humphrey Williams, William Crane, Henry Cornick, Samuel Brown,
1755	Humphrey Williams, Thomas Strode, William Crane, Henry Cornick
1756	Humphrey Williams, Thomas Strode, John Legg, William Crane, Samuel Brown,
1757	Humphrey Williams, John Short, William Crane, Henry Cornick, Samuel Brown,
1758	Humphrey Williams, John Legg, William Crane, James Gillingham
1759	Humphrey Williams, Joseph Legg, Thomas Strode, John Legg, William Crane, James Gillingham
1760	Humphrey Williams, Joseph Legg, Thomas Strode, John Legg, William Crane,

1761 Thomas Strode, William Crane, Humphrey Williams, Henry Cornick, Matthew Ford
1762 Thomas Strode, Henry Legg, William Crane, Humphrey Williams, John Legg, Matthew Ford
1763 Matthew Ford, John Legg, Thomas Strode, Robert Hallett, Henry Legg, Humphrey Williams,
1764 Humphrey Williams, Thomas Strode, Robert Hallett, Henry Legg, Henry Cornick, Matthew Ford
1765 Thomas Strode, Humphrey Williams, John Short, Henry Cornick,
1766 Humphrey Williams, Robert Hallett, John Short, Henry Cornick, Matthew Ford
1767 Humphrey Williams, John Short, Henry Cornick,
1768 Humphrey Williams, Thomas Strode, Henry Cornick, Matthew Ford
1769 Matthew Ford, Humphrey Williams, Henry Cornick, John Short,
1770 Henry Legg, Humphrey Williams, Thomas Short, Henry Cornick, John Short
1771 Henry Legg, Matthew Ford, John Short, Henry Cornick,
1772 Matthew Ford, John Short, Henry Cornick, John Chads(?)
1773 Robert Hallett, John Short, John Chads(?)
1774 Robert Hallett, John Short, John Chads(?)
1775 Matthew Ford, John Short, Henry Cornick
1776 Henry Legg, Matthew Ford, William Legg, Henry Cornick
1777 Henry Legg, Matthew Ford, Morgan Chilcott
1778 Matthew Ford, John Short
1779 Henry Legg, Matthew Ford, Job Legg
1780 Matthew Ford, Henry Cornick, Job Legg, Henry Minterne
1781 Matthew Ford, Morgan Chilcott, Henry Cornick, Job Legg
1782 Matthew Ford, Henry Minterne, Morgan Chilcott, Henry Cornick, Job Legg,
1783 Matthew Ford, Henry Minterne, Job Legg, Job Legg (name appears twice, son?)
1784 Matthew Ford, Henry Minterne, John Short
1785 Matthew Ford, Henry Minterne,
1786 Matthew Ford, Henry Minterne, John Short
1787 Matthew Ford, Henry Minterne,
1788 Matthew Ford, Henry Minterne, Job Legg
1789 Matthew Ford, Thomas Pope, Henry Minterne
1790 Matthew Ford, Henry Minterne,
1791 Matthew Ford, Henry Minterne, William Bartlett
1792 Matthew Ford, Henry Minterne, William Bartlett
1793 Henry Minterne, Thomas Pope, William Cole
1794 Henry Minterne, Thomas Pope, Matthew Ford
1795 Henry Minterne, Matthew Ford,
1796 Henry Minterne, Matthew Ford,
1797 Thomas Pope, Henry Minterne,
1798 Henry Minterne, William Bartlett
1799 Henry Minterne, John Pope
1800 Henry Minterne, John Pope
1801 Henry Minterne, John Pope
1802 John Pope, Henry Minterne, William Bartlett
1803 John Pope, Henry Minterne, William Bartlett, Joseph Bartlett
1804 John Pope, Henry Minterne, William Bartlett
1805 Henry Minterne, William Bartlett
1806 Henry Minterne, William Bartlett
1807 Henry Minterne, William Bartlett
1808 Henry Minterne, William Bartlett,
1809 Henry Minterne, William Bartlett, John Pope
1810 Henry Minterne, William Bartlett, John Pope
1811-1820 *Missing*
1821 John Pope, William Bartlett, Charles Fry
1822 John Pope, William Bartlett
1823 John Pope, William Bartlett
1824 William Bartlett, Charles Fry
1825 John Pope, William Bartlett
1826 William Bartlett, Charles Fry
1827 William Bartlett, John Short
1828 William Bartlett, John Pope
1829 John Pope, William Bartlett, John Short, Henry Cornick
1830 William Bartlett, John Short
1831 John Short, Henry Cornick
1832 John Pope, Samuel Mintern, John Short, Henry Cornick

1833 Henry Cornick, Samuel Mintern, John Short
1834 Samuel Mintern, Henry Cornick, John Short
1835 Samuel Mintern, William Bartlett, Henry Cornick, John Short
1836 Samuel Mintern, John Sims, William Bartlett, Henry Cornick, John Short
1837 Samuel Mintern, Henry Cornick, John Short,
1838 Samuel Mintern, Henry Cornick,

Appendix B

St. Giles

He was a wealthy noble born in Athens. When his parents died, he used his fortune to help the poor. To avoid his followers, because he was a miracle worker, he left Greece about 683 for France where he lived as a hermit in a cave in the diocese of Nimes. A thick thorn bush guarded the cave mouth, where he led a lifestyle so impoverished that, legend says, God sent a hind to him to nourish him with her milk.

One day, after he had lived there for several years in meditation, a royal hunting party chased the hind into Giles' cave. One hunter shot an arrow into the thorn bush hoping to hit the deer, but hit Giles in the leg instead, crippling him. The king sent doctors to care for the saint's wounds, and though Giles begged to be left alone, the king came often to see him.

From this his fame as a sage and miracle worker spread, and would-be followers gathered near the cave. The French king (Visigoth King Wamba) because of Giles' administrative ability, built the monastery of St. Gilles du Gard for these followers, and Giles became the first abbot. A small town grew up around the monastery. Upon Giles death (in about 724), his grave became a shrine and place of pilgrimage, the monastery later became a Benedictine house.

The combination of the town, monastery, shrine and pilgrims led to many handicapped beggars hoping for alms. This pilgrimage and Giles insistence that he wished to live outside the walls of the city, and his own damaged leg, led to his patronage of beggars, and cripples since begging was the only source of income for many. Hospitals and safe houses for the poor, crippled and leprous were constructed in England and Scotland, and were built so cripples could easily reach them. On their passage to Tyburn for execution, convicts were allowed to stop at Saint Giles' hospital where they were presented with a bowl of ale called Saint Giles' Bowl, "thereof to drink at their pleasure, as their last refreshing for this life".

Patronage

Over 150 churches in Great Britain are dedicated to St. Giles. He is also the patron saint of Edinburgh in Scotland

St. Giles has been claimed as saint for a multitude of needs and illnesses such as breast cancer, breast-feeding, cancer patients, cripples, disabled people, epilepsy, fear of the night, insanity, leprosy, mental illness, and sterility. He is also patron saint for many types of people and occupations including beggars, blacksmiths, handicapped people, hermits, lepers, mentally ill people, paupers, physically challenged people, poor people and spur makers; for places such as woods, forests; for rams and horses.

It would seem that he is kept very busy!

Appendix C

Rectors and Patrons of Hooke

	Patron	*Rector*
1312	Galfrid de Corington	John de Paveley *He was a rector of dubious honesty*
?		John de Stapleford (died 1348 …*was he the Rector of Stapleford at the same time?)*
1348	John Cifrewast	William Gerard
1362	John Maltravers	Henry Bilkes *Hooke and Stapleford combined on January 13*
?		John Brankard
1428	Humphry Stafford	John Richard
1459	James, Earl of Wiltshire	John Richard *There was a new patron, was it the same John Richard, his son … ?*
1476	John Coleshill, knt. and Elizabeth his wife	Robert Garnet
1513	Robert Willoughby, Lord Broke	Robert Birstal
1550		John Style *(Sir John Style according to Dorset Commissioners for Edward VI)*
?		Newman
1593		Nicholas Day *A Puritan who gave a political sermon that landed him in court: he survived*
1640		?
1650		Henry Munden BA (Morden *according to Hutchins) Interesting; the name of a local Catholic family*
1672	Lord St. John	Obadiah Thorne BA
1723	Charles, Duke of Bolton	Christopher Derby BA *also Minster of Poole!*
1735		John Johnson MA
1747		Samuel Payne BA
1791	Harry, Duke of Bolton	Samuel Lane
1827	Duke of Cleveland and Dowager Countess of Sandwich	William Floyer Cornish
1859	Duke of Cleveland and Earl of Sandwich	Arthur Pardoe BA
1862		Robert A Keedle BA
1882		I. C. Davies
1885		G. H. Jones
1888		J.L. Templer
1902	Earl of Sandwich	Richard Thomas Parker BA *Last Rector of Hooke.*

(Where there are ? for the date of induction, the year of death coincides with the induction of the next rector.)

(There is a discrepancy from the dates given in the Toller Whelme Book and those that are recorded in the church at Hooke for Reverend. Parker. The Toller Whelme book has the Reverend J. L.Templer until 1913 and the Reverend. R. T. Parker from 1914.)

Sources

Bennett W (1987) **The Toller Whelme Book** (printed by Creeds the Printers)

Hutchins J (1863) **The History and Antiquities of The County of Dorset Vol. 2,** Westminster, John Bowyer Nichols and Sons

Squibb G D (1954) **Dorset Incumbents (1542- 1731)** Reprint from *Proceedings of the Dorset Natural History and Archaeological Society*, Dorchester, Dorset Natural History and Archaeological Society

Appendix D

Police Beat Book, Hooke Police Station

Hooke Beat

Extracts from the police Beat note book, Hooke Police Station 1859-1886

Covers (1881):

Wraxall	*952 acres*	*97 population*
Hook	*1237 acres*	*154 population*
Mapperton	*804 acres*	*103 population*

(Entries here only shown for Hooke.)

Suspicious and bad characters or persons without ostensible means of gaining a livelihood, and persons who have been convicted before a magistrate:

(Columns stating Complexion, Eyes, Hair, Figure have been omitted)

Name	Age	Ht	Living	Date	Conviction
Charles Neal	40	5'9	Labourer		
Thomas Cole	25	5'5	Labourer		
William Forsey	40	5'10	Labourer(one eye closed)		Stealing wood 2 months
George Legg	45	5'8	Labourer		
William Davey	24	5'7	Labourer		Stealing wood 2 months
William Davey	27	5'7	Labourer	Jan 13 60	Profane swearing fined10s, 10s costs
George Cornick	51		Labourer	Mar 21 60	Drunkeness fined 5s, 10s costs
Joseph Davey			Labourer	Jun 12 60	Assaulting wife 3 months
Jane May	21	5'8	Dress-maker	Jul 16 60	Drunkeness 5s, 15s 6d costs
Joseph Davey				Apr 1 61	Riding without reins 6s 10d
Charles Legg			Labourer	Feb 10 62	Stealing swedes 5s
John Lankshire			Labourer	Mar 10 62	Cruelty to a cat 30s, 10s 6d costs
Samuel Cornick	19	5'7	Miller	Jun 3 62	Vagrancy 1 month
George Legg	50		Labourer	Apr 27 63	Drunkeness 5s, 2s 6d costs (an old pentioner *sic* soldier)
George Cornick	54	5'9	Labourer	Apr 29 63	Cruelty to 2 donkeys £1, 11s 6d costs
Solomon Legg	57	5'7	Labourer	Jul 20 63	Stealing 3 ash pales 14 days hard labour
Arthur Legg	32	5'5	Labourer	Jul 31 63	Stealing, Dismissed (Very abusive man)
James Davey	33	5'8	Labourer	May 23 64	Assault on Wm. Dawkins 5s, 6s costs
William Green	35	5'8	Navvy		Vagrancy 21 days (Very abusive man)
George Newman	39	5'8	Butcher	Mar 12 66	Horse straying 1s
George Newman	39	5'8	Butcher	Apr 28 66	Horse straying 8s, 7s costs
James Davey	35	5'1	Labourer	Mar 9 68	Drunk and riotous 2s, costs remitted
Sarah Ann Daws	25	5'4	Labourer	Jun 27 68	Assault Dismissed
Sarah Legg	48	5'2	Prostitute	July 27 68	Assault 2s 6d and costs
Fiennes Rendell	17	5'5	Labourer	Sep 20 68	Poaching 2s 6d and costs
William Cornick	25	5'5	unknown	Jan 25 69	Stealing 2 pheasants 2 months hard labour
Theophilus Bartlett	35	5'7	Labourer	Jul 5 69	Horse straying Caution
Now P C Ellis					
Theophilus Bartlett	35	5'7	Labourer	Sep 27 69	Donkey straying 10s
Robert Hallett	40	5'11	Miller	Sep 27 69	Donkey straying 10s
Robert Hallett	40	5'11	Miller	Dec 20 69	Donkey straying 5s, 8s and costs

Henry Bendall	20	5'10	UnderGame-keeper	Feb 18 71	Purjery (*sic*) Dismissed
James Davey	40	5'10	Labourer	Aug 28 71	Drunk and riotous Dismissed
William Gundy	59	5'10	Labourer	Feb 12 72	Poaching Bound over £1 costs
Edward Randle	50	5'6	Woodman	Nov 72	Drunk and riotous 10s and costs
Fanny Roberts	20		Labourer	Jun 3 73	Stealing a Peck(?) 14 days hard labour
John Burden	31		Horse dealer	Sep 29 73	Poaching £3, 8s costs
Henry Burden	60		Horse dealer	Sep 29 73	Poaching £3, 8s costs
John Tight	20		Horse dealer	Sep 29 73	Poaching £3, 8s costs
William Davey	38	5'9	Labourer and poacher	Mar 15 75	Causing a nuisance and refusing to quit 50s, 9s costs (bad character)
James Belling	43	5'9	Labourer	Sep 29 75	Poaching One month
John Fry	50	5'8	Labourer	Sep 29 75	Poaching one month
John Fry	50	5'8	Labourer	Sep 29 75	Poaching fined £2
Robert Hallett	46	5'10	Miller's baker	Oct 25 76	Selling bread without weights 10s
John Davey	50	5'8	Farmer	Sep 29 76	Neglecting to report cows with Foot and Mouth disease 10s
James Davey	44	5'10	Labourer	Aug 7 77	Drunk and riotous 21 days hard labour
Charles Cleal	21	5'6	Labourer	Nov 28 77	Poaching 10s and costs
Edward Mintern	49	5'9	Carter	Feb 11 78	Cruelty and ill treating mare £4, 6s costs
Edward Davey	50	6'	Poacher	Mar 23 78	Drunkeness and refusing to quit a licensed premises £1, 8s costs and 1 month hard labour
Elizabeth Mintern	46	5'	Farmer	Jul 29 78	Cows straying on highway 3s, 7s costs
Edward Davey	48	5'11	Labourer	Oct 17 78	Breach of peace Bound over for 3 months 12s costs
Edwin Hoddinott	34	5'8	Dairyman	Apr 7 79	Keeping dog without licence 8s, 8s costs
Sarah Gale	16	4'6	Live with her father	Mar 6 80	Stealing turnips 6d and value 3d
James Higgins	44	5'8	Labourer	Nov 7 81	Setting fire to a cottage Acquitted at Assizes (died Dec 31 1881)
Charlotte Neal	67	5'4	Kept by Parish	Sep 13 82	Stealing faggotts 10s
Charlotte Neal	67	5'4	Kept by Parish	Oct 31 82	Stealing a carpet Dismissed with a caution
Edward Davey	53	6'	Labourer	Jun 10 85	Stealing fowls 3 months (Edward Davey came from Bridport to Hook June 1884; the Grand Jury found no bill.) Dead*: entry crossed out.*
Frederick Symes	18	5'9	Labourer	Sep 16 85	Attempted rape Committed for trial
George Pottle	32	5'7	Game keeper for the Earl of Sandwich	Aug 5 86	Keeping 2 dogs without licence 2s6d, 7s costs

Return of Public and Beer Houses

			How conducted
Hook	Masons Arms	Charles Legg Randle	
Hook	(Beer House?)	Jacob Mintern	
Hook	Masons Arms	Charles Legg Randle	fined 6s costs 9s Jan 17 1870
Hook	Paulet Arms	James Oliver (original entry Bailey crossed out)	Orderly

NB no entry in Police Beat book for Charles Legg Randle on Jan. 17 1870, was this a licensing offence?

(Entries copied by Duncan Harris Jan 7 1997.)

Appendix E

Hooke Residents Occupations 1995

There were 80 adults and 40 children under 18.

Agricultural engineer
Aquacare firm (2)
Builder
Chef
Computer software designer (2)
Cowman
Customs and Excise officer
Dentist
Educational Trust Manager
Electrical contractor
Equestrian Centre inspector
Farmer (4)
Fish bait breeder
Fish farm manager
Fish farm owner
Furniture designer
Go-kart Centre proprietor (3)
Guesthouse proprietor.
Head teacher (3)
Horologist
House broker
Lorry driver
Midwife
Retired (18)
Sales manager
School odd job man
Security officer
Shop assistant
Solicitor
Stable owner
Teacher/lecturer (3)
Teaching assistant
Woodsman

The remainder of adults were house-wives or house-husbands.

Appendix F

Major Charles Herbert Mullins V.C.

Major C H Mullins VC
Imperial Light Horse of Johannesberg
(At Hooke Court for convalescence: July 20 – 24, 1901)

He joined the Imperial Light Horse at Pietermaritzberg as a Captain on September 19th 1899. Captain Mullins was awarded the Victoria Cross for his action at the *Battle of Elandslaagte,* South Africa during the Boer War on October 21st 1899. At a most critical moment when the advance was checked by severe fire at point-blank range, Captain Mullins and another officer (Johnston R.) gallantly rushed forward under very heavy fire and rallied the men, thus enabling the decisive flanking movement to be carried out. Captain Mullins was wounded in the right breast during the action. He went to hospital in Ladysmith.

He was at Ladysmith during the siege from January 1st to April 9th 1900. He caught enteric fever. He rejoined at Elandslaagte and went from there to Capetown and Kimberley. He was engaged in the relief of Mafeking under Mahon and dangerously wounded in the spine on May 13th 1900. He was taken back to Mafeking after the relief. After 6 weeks he went to Deelfontein Hospital where the bullet was removed on August 8th 1900. He was invalided to England in *Grahamstown* in April 1901. He was at Hooke Court with his brother from July 20th –July 24th 1901.

He was also awarded the C. M. G. (Companion of the Order of St. Michael and St. George).

His brother, the Reverend R. J. Mullins left the column at Senekal to nurse Captain Mullins' dangerous wound, tended him on the field and remained with him at Deelfontein, in England and during his convalescence at Hooke Court.

Captain Mullins was later promoted to Major.

He died on 24th May 1916 at Johannesburg and is buried at Grahamstown Old Cemetry.

Sources

Harris D (2003) **Officers South Africa 1900-1901. 1902.** Hooke Dorset (Copies are held at Beaminster Museum and the Military Museum in London)

Lys I (2000) **Victoria Crosses of the Anglo-Boer War**